About the Author

The V. Rev. Dr. David Smith is a priest of the Antiochian Orthodox Church, Diocese of Ottawa. He is a licensed nursing home administrator, and operates a nursing home in Oswego, New York. He lives in Syracuse with his wife and four children.

CHRISTIANITY and PLEASURE

by

Father David R. Smith

Regina Orthodox Press
Salisbury, Massachusetts

CHRISTIANITY and PLEASURE

ISBN # 978-1-928653-32-5

© 2008 Father David R. Smith

Regina Orthodox Press
PO Box 5288
Salisbury MA 01952

reginaorthodoxpress.com

Acknowledgements

My deepest thanks must be extended to Fr. Juvenaly of St. Tikhon's Seminary library for his helpful suggestions, and to Fr. Gregory Murphy for the deep conversations that took place while we tackled, almost weekly, a frustrating and pleasurable problem. The Bible Study group at St. George's Orthodox Church in Utica listened to every chapter patiently and offered many helpful insights.

Presbytera Donna did more than any writer could expect, with her frank criticism, opposing viewpoints, and unending support.

To my wife Donna.

"I wish this moment would last forever."

TABLE OF CONTENTS

x

1

FOUR DEFINITIONS OF PLEASURE

*   *   *

In my years as a follower of Jesus Christ, I have come to discover that my relationship with the things I consider pleasurable (and also, conversely, not pleasurable) most determines the quality of my relationship with God. When I think of only getting what I want, or more accurately, when I don't think at all, my soul shrivels, and God seems absent. When, on the other hand, I determine to find pleasure in those things that feed my relationship with God, my soul feasts. I have a sense, in fact, that I could describe almost every moment of my life based on that particular moment's definition, attitude toward, and relationship to pleasure. Perhaps it's that way with you, too. Think about it. We all gravitate toward those things that bring us pleasure, and try to avoid those things that do not. This applies whether we're speaking about the "higher pleasures," like learning, prayer, worship, and sacrifice, or the more base and meaningless pleasures.

    We are often unaware that pleasure is the engine that drives us. Without this awareness, we lunge from activity to activity with no sense of what we really want, no sense of what really gives our lives joy. I can remember, in my younger years, basing my opinion of what was pleasurable on the thoughts of others. What music I liked. Where I spent my time. How I dressed. But when I began to really think about the issue, to decide what I wanted for myself, I could see that what other people were telling me to enjoy was not necessarily what I actually enjoyed. I embarked, at that moment, upon the process of arriving at of my own definition of pleasure.

My hope is that we discover how seeking a Christian definition of pleasure can give us the attitude we need to cultivate a healthy and joyous relationship with God.

Is Christianity All Pleasure or No Pleasure at all?

Some people, I've discovered, treat Christianity and pleasure only as extremes. It begs the question: Is Christianity all pleasure or no pleasure at all? Of course when I say "all pleasure," I mean good things. Fulfillment, peace, fellowship, family. And when I say "no pleasure," well, "no pleasure" is another thing entirely.

First, I'll look at the "all pleasure" side. I became a serious Christian by listening to the preaching of Billy Graham, and I've listened to many of his sermons. After having heard him many times, I think most of his evangelistic preaching can be summed up this way:

1) You're not happy. You may think you are, but you're not.
2) I have good news, though. Jesus will make you happy.

I do not mean to ridicule the ministry of Billy Graham. Thousands besides me have stepped through the front door of the church because of his preaching. But what happens if I'm not happy after giving my life to Jesus? What if I don't really feel fulfilled? Does our Lord guarantee that everyone who becomes a Christian also becomes happy? When I put it so bluntly, it certainly sounds ridiculous. Billy Graham would never describe the gospel in this way. Yet, since I've been a priest, how many times have I had people come to talk to me because they're not happy? Nine times out of ten, those who complain that they're not happy believe it's the Church's, or God's fault. In so many words they say to me, "I believe in God, but it's not helping. Look at me, I'm unhappy!"

For many years, I found myself trying to "fix" this problem. I'd give advice. "Repent of your sins," I'd say. "Get your wife to join you in church," I'd suggest. "Resign from the parish counsel," is one splendid idea. Or perhaps I'd just say, "you have to pray more." In almost all cases, my advice wouldn't work. Then what? In my mind, I'd think, "This person is not disciplined enough to enjoy the spiritual life. If he were, he'd be happy." But – doesn't every program say that? Alcoholic's Anonymous says that, all the diets say that, every psychologist says it: "if the program's not working, it's because you're not doing it right." Is Christianity just another psycho-social program? If you pray enough and "work the program," will happiness and fulfillment always result? If someone is not happy, can his fellow Christians always give him some advice about following the system better that will make him find the happiness he seeks?

Most Christians would answer "yes." It's the wrong answer, but it's what most people believe. This attitude is widespread because most people seek a kind of shallow pleasure above all things, and they've come to consider Christianity as just one more part of that search. Preachers support this attitude. Many sermons swing back and forth from proclaiming the gospel to teaching about happiness, balance, how to pay off your credit cards, how to have a good marriage, etc. They swing back and forth so quickly, in fact, that the two different sermons become one sermon – the gospel of Jesus Christ becomes the good news of psychological stability and happiness.

Is it possible not to fall into the trap of thinking this way? Certainly. But it takes careful meditation on the issue of pleasure, so that we can really learn what it means to give our lives to God. When you surrender your life to God, you will not get all the things you want. You will get some things you don't want. I know, for instance, many priests who pastor miserable and unrewarding churches, and they are unhappy. But they remain in their places because that's what God has called them to, and they want to obey God more than they want to have the pleasure of big salaries and adulation. If you said to one of them right now, "Does Christianity make everyone happy?" they would sigh and cross themselves. But each would be, and remain, faithful to God.

Now let's look at the "no pleasure" side. I began to notice after I entered the church that I would occasionally meet good Christians who are the opposite of happy. You know people like this. The man who believes that Christianity must contain no pleasure at all. The woman who believes that Christians are following Christ only when they're miserable. The monk who sneers at everyone he meets. No music except music from the church. No TV, of course, or movies. No sports. No newspapers, just books of spiritual value. No conversation that is not spiritual in nature. No radio, except for religious programs, or perhaps classical music. Tiny amounts of food, only drink water. Anything that looks like it may involve pleasure is avoided and ridiculed. Happiness is just another word for underestimating sin. Laughter is nothing more than the braying of demons.

Sometimes these folks are hard to take, but admit it, if you don't admire them, at least a little, it's because you won't face the fact that their "all for God" lifestyle challenges you in an uncomfortable way. Most Christians will admit that Christianity needs these kinds of people, and looks to them as leaders and as examples. But have you ever tried to imitate them? I know I have. I was close to a monk who was a very simple and single minded man. I wanted to be like him (or more accurately, I wanted people to admire me the way I admired him). Just after I met him, I submitted myself to a particularly severe Lenten fast: no TV, no newspaper, no books, no radio in the car, along with the normal Lenten disciplines of the Orthodox Church. That year, as Pascha was approaching, I often caught myself daydreaming about the good things that would finally be mine. The fast would soon be over – at last! The deprivation would end, and I could finally enjoy life again! Several parishioners came over to our home after the Resurrection Liturgy, and were amazed at how happy I was that Pascha had come. But was that Paschal joy? Not in the least! I had denied myself pleasures of life that I normally enjoyed in moderation in order to make myself into someone I was not, and Pascha was simply the limit I had set for myself after which I could stop trying.

Certainly, the church gives us the Lenten fast in order to put us in touch with the requirements of spiritual discipline, and brings us face-to-face with the resistance we have to giving our lives over to God. But I missed that lesson, because my mind was focused on the pleasures I had given up. Lent that year was not a time of learning and self revelation, it was like waiting at a red light. I just sat there until the calendar told me I could move on.

The saints were "all or nothing" Christians. We look to them through lovely and comforting icons in the church, but imagine St. Athanasius the Great walked into the room where you're reading this right now. What would he say to you? "You're a wonderful Christian, I'm proud of you!" Probably not. He'd would, if you're anything like me, most likely start to hit you with his staff. He'd tell you to stop reading books and start to weep for your sins. He'd tell you that you should go to church every day and lie on the ground outside and cry out to God for forgiveness. Would he be correct? Absolutely!

Would you do it, though? Would you follow his advice? I agree that the church needs the "all or nothing" people, and I greatly admire them. But did God intend that everyone in the church would be "all or nothing," and Hell would be the only option for the rest of us?

That's the question. Some believe that Christianity is all pleasure, and some believe that Christianity is no pleasure at all. Which is it? The easy response would be to say that Christians live somewhere in the middle. An answer like this might say, "Enjoy the things of this world, but don't be enslaved by them." That sounds like a good conclusion at first, but when we look at the subject a little more, we'll see that that's not really a satisfactory answer. Christianity does not call us to a life of teetering between the restrictive rules of God and the fun of the devil. The Christian life does not resemble the speed limit, where if it's 65 miles per hour, I know I can pass a speed trap at 74 and get away with it. It's not a balance, it's not cruise control. It's loving God with all your heart, mind, and body.

Living the Christian life is a matter of understanding how some pleasure draws us toward God and other pleasure takes us away from Him.

Four Ways to Define Pleasure

We're going to look at pleasure through four different definitions, and we'll use these definitions as the basis for the rest of our discussion. Pleasure is such a big term, we need to look at it from a variety of angles.

First, pleasure can be defined as "desire fulfilled." I get this definition from St. Maximos the Confessor, who wrote at length about the subject of pleasure in *The Philokalia*[1]. Sometimes when I read the church fathers, they seem to use the word "pleasure" to describe only worldly things – the word, to them, is consistently negative. St. Maximos does not do this, and that's why I find his writing particularly helpful. He speaks of "meaningless" pleasure[2], and "divine" pleasure[3], and makes it clear that we can take delight in God without being afraid of delight itself. After all, many people take pleasure in sacred things – the church, the liturgy,

---

[1] Lorenzo Scupoli, *Unseen Warfare, Being the Spiritual Combat and Path to Paradise of Lorenzo Scupoli*, ed. St. Nocodemus of the Holy Mountain, rev. Theophan the Recluse, trans. Kadloubovsky and Palmer (London, Faber and Faber, 1952), 244
[2] Ibid, 244
[3] Ibid, 244

the music, icons, and prayer – the pleasure they experience cannot be bad simply because it's pleasurable.

If pleasure is "desire fulfilled," we can experience a holy pleasure when we achieve our desire of knowing God, or come close to it. The key is to desire good things that lead us toward that goal – if we do, then we will take pleasure in pursuing and achieving them. But how do we do that?

First, we have to admit that we all desire both good things and bad things. Sometimes we're afraid to say what the bad ones are. We don't express desires when we realize at some level that our desires do nothing other than to point to our greed and selfishness. If your confessor asked you what you desire in life, you may say something like, "I want to know God's will, and then to have the strength to do it." It's a Sunday school answer. It's the kind of thing people say when they go to confession. But what, really, do most people desire? To have unlimited amounts of money, the drive a big car, to have others look at them with admiration, and the like? Well, yes. I'll tell you, more Christians desire those things above their desire to know the will of God and have the strength to do it. I'm not saying that no one wants to do the will of God, not at all. But all of us have hidden desires that keep us away from the pleasure of knowing God.

This is the key to understanding desire, and desire's relationship to pleasure. We all continually desire many different, and often contradictory, things at the same time. We desire them because we believe that they will bring us pleasure when we achieve, or own them. How can we reconcile these contradictions? How can I say I want to do God's will at the same time as I live my life according to nothing but my own will?

St. Paul recognized the same struggle when he wrote, "But I see another law in my members, warring against the law of my mind, and bringing me into captivity to the law of sin which is in my members. O wretched man that I am! Who will deliver me from this body of death?"[4] The great Apostle

---

[4] Romans 7:23-24. All Biblical Citations are from the New King James version.

describes his contradictory desires as coming from different sources - which indeed they do. We need to figure out how to sort these contradictory desires.

We'll search for the answer in chapter two, "What Do You Want," chapter three, "Crucify Your Mind," and chapter four, "Be Thinkful."

Second, I define pleasure as that moment at which you might say to yourself: "I wish this moment would last forever." Our first definition, that pleasure is desire fulfilled, focuses on the future. But pleasure happens in the immediate as well, it happens when we come to a situation, a circumstance, an attitude that makes us feel like we've arrived. I was the pastor of a church where a group of parishioners would come to my home every Sunday after the liturgy, and we would talk about the spiritual life all afternoon. This tradition continued for many months. I can remember often sitting at my dining room table with the most contented feeling. I was surrounded by good people and good conversation. My wife bore the brunt of the preparations – but she enjoyed those afternoons as much as I did, and she worked hard to make sure that the good conversation always took place around good food, and that the kids were playing nicely. It was like a vacation every week – and although I didn't think about it in so many words, if you had asked me at the time I would have said that I wished the experience, or at least that feeling of contentment, would last forever.

Sometimes this sensation of contentment comes from something good, something that fills you with a longing to be close to God, like when you visit a monastery and find yourself daydreaming about staying there forever. Sometimes it comes from something meaningless, like people who wish deep down that they could have enough money to do nothing all the time. Like someone who would drink all the time if he didn't need to hold down a job.

The longing for lasting contentment can come from bad or good pleasures, but they both share something in common – permanency. They both show a longing for permanency in this world (and in the next as well), which is impossible.

We will look at this in chapter five, "The Opposite of Pleasure is Pain," chapter six, "We Have No Home in This World," chapter seven, "Heaven Begins Today," and chapter eight, "We Learn to Love Pleasure Before We Know We're Learning to Love Pleasure."

Third, I define pleasure as an attitude of joy, release, and comfort. I have a job that is very stressful and busy at times. I have a tradition of having a cup of coffee at 9:30 am, and this gets me through the morning and lunch time. Around three in the afternoon, I lose steam rapidly and really need another cup of coffee to regain my energy and focus. Sometimes I'll go out to a premium coffee place in our village to get a cup. The coffee is delicious. The first sip slows me down. I stop and taste it, and might even be heard sincerely thanking God. Then, each subsequent sip stokes the fire, at first slow and luscious, and brings me back to life. Is this an example of my first definition of pleasure, the fulfillment of a desire? Not really. If you asked me to make a list of the things I desire most in life, I don't think "afternoon coffee at work" would even make the list. Is it an example of my second definition, a moment that I wish would last forever? No. I really want time to keep on moving toward the moment when I can go home.

This definition of the word "pleasure" aims at the little things in life. Driving on a beautiful day, a favorite TV program, a nice little meal, reading a book, a lovely day of interesting weather, or any one of a hundred other commonplace and daily events and responsibilities.

We will look at this definition in chapter nine, "The Lord's Prayer and Pleasure," and chapter ten, "Popular Entertainment."

Fourth, I define pleasure as communion with another person. This kind of pleasure embraces all the other definitions - it can be top on your list of things you desire in life, it can involve moments that you wish would last forever, and it can express itself in a hundred little interactions that make life rich and joyful. I added this fourth definition because communion with another person involves the deepest kind of pleasure, and is the only kind of pleasure that can be rich and full in spite of involving copious amounts of pain and frustration. Any parent of a teenager knows what I mean.

I know a nursing home that had a particularly difficult resident. He was selfish, inappropriate, filthy, and loud. Every member of the staff hated him. But when he died, many staff from the nursing home showed up at his funeral, crying great streams of grief. Sometimes, intense communion with another person, even when it's intensely bad, gives us a kind of pleasure and a deep experience of love.

I also added a fourth definition because this fourth is the definition of pleasure that can describe an abiding relationship with God, or more than that. Definition number one can describe the pleasure of a relationship with God, as when I might say, "I desire a relationship with God." But definition four describes something better. Holier. More intense. Pursuing a relationship with God is not the same thing as pursuing God Himself. In the spiritual disciplines of the church, I seek a relationship with God. But in prayer, the most directly connected-to-God of the spiritual disciplines, I seek God Himself. It's like the difference between learning about a person and meeting that person. Of course, you have to learn things about someone to really know him. But the pleasure of knowing about God (which is, after all, significantly pleasurable) differs from that experience of prayer when the divine presence surrounds and fills you. Am I right?

Read or re-read the book *Courage to Pray* by Anthony Bloom[5]. Again and again, he describes prayer in one word: encounter. With "encounter," even a sigh can be a prayer. Without "encounter," even a Paschal liturgy is only a form of cultural entertainment. This is the central pleasure of Christ-

---

[5] Anthony Bloom, *Courage to Pray* (New York, St Vladimir's Seminary Press, 1997)

ianity, that we commune with God Himself: "the immensity of our vocation is to share the divine nature."[6]

Ascetics are the highest expression of this kind of pleasure; they seek to commune continually with God. Bloom tells us that good ascesis is a sure pathway to pleasure: "in ascesis we are not primarily seeking the joy of an encounter with God, but the deep transformation that God alone can work in us, that we are prepared, as the Church Fathers said, to give our blood in order to receive the Spirit."[7] The ascetic doesn't seek a relationship with God, but God Himself, and the pain of the ascetic discipline to which God has called him only intensifies the pleasure of the communion.

I bet you never thought of ascetics as pleasure seekers, but indeed, they seek the pleasure of communing with God above everything else!

Unfortunately, like the other pleasures, we can seek communion with other people for evil reasons. Some use other people as nothing but sources to satisfy a restless lust for competition. I had a supervisor at one of the jobs I've held who was like this. Everything – how clean he kept his office, how early he could come to work, how quickly he could drive somewhere, how well he made coffee – everything was a competition to him. Of course, there are many other kinds of lust as well. There are those for whom relationships with other people contain nothing good, altruistic, holy, or stable. I had the opportunity to speak recently to a woman who was contemplating a third marriage – and she wasn't an old woman. I told her that I would not celebrate a wedding for her, because she obviously had a very serious problem with how she used, and let herself be used by, men. She wanted to know what I meant.

"Do you think you've changed significantly since your last divorce, or even since the first one?" I asked her.

"No," she said. At least she was honest.

---

[6] Ibid, 6
[7] Ibid, 36

I asked her another question. "With the fact in mind that you're the same person who has failed at marriage twice already, and your fiancé has failed once, do you really think that marriage number three will be good, stable, and holy?"

She didn't answer me, because the right answer would have been, "Not a chance." But of course she wouldn't have given that answer, since the giddiness that comes when immature people meet a new friend had stopped up her ears.

But let me ask this: in the time before and just after their wedding, were those two experiencing the pleasure that comes from communion with another person? Yes, certainly. But the communion would not survive in the long run. It might not even survive a year.

We'll look at pleasure as communion with another person in chapter eleven, "The Highest Pleasure," and end with, "The Essence of the Matter."

Now we've started and we know where we want to go. Our goal is to examine the issue of pleasure, using the four definitions, in such a way that we do not allow our constant longing for pleasure to contaminate our relationship with God. Let's get started with the most basic question of all – what do you want?

2

WHAT DO YOU WANT?

*   *   *

We'll start our discussion of pleasure with St. Maximos' definition that pleasure is "desire fulfilled." If this is true, the real question then becomes: what do you desire? If pleasure is linked closely to desire, we can change what we find pleasurable by changing what we find desirable.

Or, more simply put, what do you want?

Before we answer this question, we need to consider that everyone defines pleasure at several different levels – that is, we want different things at the same time. How do we distinguish between these various desires? How can we use our good sense to pursue the anticipated pleasure that will give us the most joy in life?

One day I came home from work, and I really wanted to rest because it had been a hard day and a difficult drive home. I sat on the couch and turned on the TV, which was what I really desired to do that evening. But I had forgotten that one of the kids had a game he wanted me to see. Of course, I turned off the TV and I went to the game. I wanted to see him play a sport that was important to him more than I wanted to rest and watch TV. I also knew that at the game I would not say to myself, "A better man would be at home watching TV," but if I had stayed home, I'd think several times during the TV program "I'm a bad father."

However, even though I decided to go to the game (and could honestly say that the game is where I wanted to be), while I watched my son play, I also wished I could have been home relaxing.

So can you see the motivation behind my going to the game? I wanted to spend time with my family, and I wanted to see my son play. But I also didn't want to feel bad about myself.

At every moment in our lives, we have competing desires, and competing motivations for following one of our desires over another. We must decide, then, which desires should dictate what we actually do. Which desires should come out on top. Good desires vs. those that should be set aside.

The scriptures contain a valuable story that illustrates the issue of competing desires. When King David had become the king of a unified Hebrew nation, he sent his armies forth to conquer new lands while he stayed behind in Jerusalem. In II Samuel 11:1-22, we read of a temptation that came to David. He saw Bathsheba from the roof of his palace, invited her to come for a visit, got her pregnant, and (after attempting to cover up his sin) had her husband killed. Others also died during the execution of the plan to kill her husband. This sounds like the behavior of a terrible and godless person, doesn't it? And yet we read in II Samuel 7:3 – just four chapters before the Bathsheba story – that David asked the prophet Nathan what he should do about building the Lord a house of worship, and Nathan replied, "Go, do all that is in your heart, for the Lord is with you."

This is why they call David a prophet – when he asked the greatest prophet of his time what to do, the prophet told him that the Lord would speak directly to the king's heart. He didn't need a prophet, an intermediary. King David was like those of us living in the time after Christ's

Resurrection, who possess the Holy Spirit and are spoken to directly by God. But how could someone who heard those words from Nathan the prophet in chapter seven commit the terrible sins of chapter eleven?

You and I both know that it's very easy to sin, even after times when you've drawn so close to God that you feel the same fire in the spirit that the prophets must have felt. Even when the Holy Spirit fills us to overflowing, we never escape the attraction of the most base and ridiculous sins. Sinning is easy. King David's story is much more than a tawdry spectacle of political indiscretion, because his sad story is the same story as anyone who will listen to it. In fact, I would go so far as to say that you who are reading this now have probably never committed sins like King David's sins in Second Samuel chapter eleven only because you don't have the power that he had to get away with things like that. If you did, you would have.

So King David committed these terrible sins, adultery followed by murder, but why? He did it because he wanted to. During the whole episode of adultery, followed by the days of attempted cover up, followed by the carefully orchestrated murder, David wanted Bathsheba. He wanted power and pleasure. But he wanted to do God's will as well. He wanted to do God's will like any prophet/king would want to do — but he didn't. He must have, at times during those days, asked himself what in the world he was doing. Part of him said, "It's OK, you're the king," and another part said, "You are despicable and a disappointment to God."

So with us. We all live every day with competing desires vying for attention virtually all at once. The first thing we need to realize is that God knows this. He's planned for it with a strategy called repentance and forgiveness.

Let me ask you a question. What good thing has survived from the episode of David and Bathsheba? All the people from that time are dead, and various parties in the story have no more stake in retribution or accusation. But what has survived? Every day, Orthodox Christians recite the prayer that has emerged from the David and Bathsheba tragedy: "Have mercy upon me, O God, according to your loving kindness; according to the multitude of your tender mercies, blot out my transgressions."[8] We know that this Psalm is specific to this particular episode because of the preamble, which we rarely or never hear, "To the Chief Musician. A Psalm of David when Nathan the prophet went to him, after he had gone in to Bathsheba." The compiler of the Psalms wanted us to remember that the greatest expression of repentance in the scriptures, the fifty-first Psalm, resulted from the terrible series of sins we read about in Second Samuel. King David eventually recognized his sin, his need for God, and repented for what he had done. He repented with a cry so genuine that it has touched many generations of God-lovers.

You have competing notions of desire and pleasure working in your mind right now. You may turn to the one that came from God, or not. But I have good news. If you get it wrong, God will forgive. He'll never stop calling, even when time and time again you do not choose what He wants you to choose.

Eternity

We know that when we choose wrong, we have the opportunity to repent, and God forgives. But what can we do to make the right choice more often than we do now? One answer is to look at the impact of every moment of our lives in terms of its relation to eternity. Can eternity influence the way that we live our lives on a day-to-day basis?

In the Old Testament book of Ecclesiastes, the Patriarch Solomon (incidentally, a son that came of King David's liaison with Bathsheba) gave us an answer to this when he wrote, "He has made everything beautiful in its time. Also He has put eternity in their hearts."[9] Eternity in their hearts. The "their," by the way, means you. God has put

---

[8] Psalm 51:1
[9] Ecclesiastes 3:11

eternity in your heart. When you look inside yourself, you can find it there. Eternity and space. You make the discovery that life has gone on long before you came along and will continue long after you've died. All of it may not seem beautiful to you, but in its time, He makes all things beautiful.

If this perspective directed every aspect of your life, wouldn't you become a person who consistently desires good things? All you need to do is nurture the eternity that God has placed in your heart. You find God's will there, not only for yourself, but for the whole world throughout history.

But the word "eternity" does not only refer to time. We do not understand the concept of eternity when we define it simply by adding all the time that has come before us, plus the present, plus all the time that is yet to come. "Eternity" does not consist of a sum of time, but a procession of life. God makes (as Solomon reminds us) "everything beautiful in its time." What does this mean? What does it mean but that God has given time to the world as a means of traveling toward the perfect destination of His will? This is why time exists, to serve eternity. Eternity is a progression, a departure and an arrival point, a divine consciousness, a goal toward which all things move. We do not measure time when we use the word "eternity," but we measure the enormity of God's perfect will.

Keeping your mind on eternity is the same as keeping your mind on God, practically speaking (I am not, of course, equating eternity with God). Notice that I didn't say God's *will* - that's different than God himself. Eternity as a concept cannot be grasped by men. We cannot imagine eternity when we force it to refer only to time, but we can strive to discover it when we define it as the world's progression toward the perfect will of the Creator. It is God who inhabits eternity, and God who defines it. It is God who created eternity, because it is God who created everything whose motion, life, death, and decay feeds the passing of time. We can't imagine God, but we can embrace Him, and seek to accomplish His will.

We must embrace eternity, then, as a person, not a concept. As a person, eternity provides us with a point of reference and with relationship. In my example of attending my son's game, if I had asked myself which way of spending time would have more value in eternity, I would most certainly (as I did) go to the game. But what if my perspective on eternity did not help me to arrive at a good answer? Suppose my son didn't get to play at the game I attended, and he was embarrassed that I was there? Suppose he came home thankful that I had missed his game and appreciated the fact that we could sit and watch a little TV together and not talk about his sports shortcomings at all?

It's different when I ask God what I should do, because I can hear His voice in the Holy Spirit. He knows eternity. He has a perspective that I do not and cannot have. When I look at eternity standing next to God, hand in hand, I gain many insights into the way in which I can bring pleasure to my life and to the lives of others than if I just "imagine eternity" on my own.

Let's say that a parishioner comes to me and asks me to take a "shortcut" or make some kind of exception about something, as sometimes happens. Perhaps I like this person, and I can understand the problem he's having, and I think I might agree to cut a corner or two. But when I call the bishop to ask his permission, he says no. He understands that the entire church would suffer if the particular rule or tradition I want to set aside was lost, and he tells me to refuse the parishioner's request and adhere to the normal practice of the church. What's the difference between the bishop and me? Perspective. He looks at the whole church, at the whole diocese, even the whole of history, and judges any request from that perspective. So with God and us. Just as the bishop has a perspective that the priest does not, so God has a perspective on eternity that we do not. We might decide on a on a course of action based on our understanding of eternity, but how would we know the decision is correct? We can't grasp eternity. Only God can.

I Want God

When I go back to the question of what I want, I find that all answers fall short in some way unless the answer I give is "God." I want God. I don't want to figure out His will, I don't want to figure out eternity, I don't want to add stuff to my life in order to deepen my relationship with God. No. I want God. That's right, I said I don't want to deepen my relationship with God. Pursuing a relationship with God and pursuing God Himself are often very different things. Of course, when we go to church in order to deepen our relationship with God, we do in fact find it deeper for the effort. But the church is not God. We must go to the church, an external behavior, in order to help us draw near to God, an inner reality.

I must be careful in making this point. History has seen religious movements that take what I have just said to mean that the external realities of the Christian faith are discretionary. They might say, "We don't need to go to church as long as we seek after God," or, "We don't need to be baptized as long as we're born again in our hearts," or, "Holy Communion is not important because I can commune with God in other ways." This is silly. It makes God - forgive me for saying - into nothing but a function of the mind. It's like a friend who doesn't call or write for years and then says, "Sorry I haven't called or written, but I've thought about you often." What can you say? Hearing those words does little to renew the relationship that was destroyed when you realized that your friend was ignoring your calls and letters, it does little to soothe the old pain of rejection. Thinking about God is useless as the sole pathway to knowing God. Many pathways, the church and the disciplines of the church, have been established and used by Christians for hundreds of years. Suddenly, the last two hundred years, we assume that we are good enough that we can skip over them and arrive at the same destination? We can't.

Do you want God? Use the church to find Him. Don't forget the church, the way, and don't forget God, the destination.

Jacob's Example

The story of the Patriarch Jacob in the Old Testament illustrates a progression from religious formality to knowing God. A progression from thinking about the idea of God in religious ritual to knowing God Himself.

To those who reject the church, I have to say: when you stay all the way to the end of Jacob's story, you'll see that his religious formality didn't stop when he came to know God. As a matter of fact, it increased!

Jacob's story begins in Genesis chapter 27, when his father was very old and had decided that he didn't have long to live. The father told Jacob's older brother to go hunting and prepare a good meal so that he might bestow a final blessing, a blessing of the first born son. Jacob's mother overheard what the old man said, and came up with a little plan: she prepared her own delicious meal and had Jacob take it to his father, disguised as the older brother, so that Jacob might receive the blessing of the first born.

The plan worked. Jacob was blessed by his father before his older brother had even returned from hunting. Here, we see how Jacob valued religious formality as a part of his family and ethnic traditions. He wanted the blessing that his father would give to the first born son. Why? Because it would make his life easy? Because he could, from that day onward, tell his brother what to do and his brother would have to do it (as the blessing implied)? I'll tell you, if you remember this story at all you know that neither of these things happened. As a matter of fact, when his older brother found out what Jacob had done, he told everyone that he would kill Jacob as soon as the father died. Jacob had to flee, and he went to serve his uncle for many years. Then, when he ran from his uncle like a fugitive he returned to his home and his brother with his forehead to the ground. A fat lot of good the blessing of Isaac did for Jacob – at least from a non-eternal perspective! Practically speaking, the blessing was nothing more than a point of religious formality to the family, but it was a point of religious formality that Jacob and his family deemed very important.

Of course, the blessing was very important to God as well. But I don't think Jacob thought about God at all early in his life. He was what I call a "functional atheist," a person whose every behavior indicates no belief in the existence of God. In Jacob's case, he thought he was living entirely by his own wits. When his father asked him how he so quickly returned from hunting, Jacob replied, "Because the Lord your God caused it to happen to me."[10] What's the key word here? "Your." Isaac's God was not Jacob's god. He needed to think up a lie quickly, and he used what he thought was the old man's superstitions as his excuse.

The next instance of Jacob's religious attitude was when he fled from his brother. Jacob's mother told him not to wait until the death of his father to see if the older brother would carry out his threat, but to leave immediately. Jacob left, but not without inner conflict. How was he supposed to collect on the blessing he had received if his brother's threat forced him to leave his home? As he journeyed, he stopped in "a certain place"[11] and lay down to sleep with a stone as his pillow. He had a dream of a ladder extending from earth to heaven, with angels ascending and descending and the Lord God standing at the top. God assured Jacob that the blessing he received did indeed have great power: "I am the Lord God of Abraham thy father, and the God of Isaac; the land whereon thou liest, to thee will I give it, and to thy seed; and thy seed shall be as the dust of the earth."[12]

Now I want to take a close look at a couple indications that Jacob still did not know God, but only related to the idea of God through religious ritual. First of all, Jacob did not say anything to God. He listened to God's words,

[10] Genesis 27:20
[11] Genesis 28:11
[12] Genesis 28:13-14a

woke up, and spoke to himself, "Surely the Lord is in the place; and I knew it not."[13] But he said nothing to God. Jacob was at the point in the spiritual life when a person fears, but does not love, God. Jacob was too afraid of God in his dream to say anything. Second, Jacob did not entirely believe the word he heard from God. On the morning after the dream, Jacob set up his pillow as an altar and anointed it with oil. He made a covenant – but not with God. Who would you say Jacob's covenant was with? "If God will be with me, and will keep me in this way that I go, and will give me bread to eat, and raiment to put on, so that I come again to my father's house in peace; then shall the Lord be my God."[14] Jacob sure knew how to hedge his bets! If God was real, and did what He said He would do, then Jacob promised to serve Him. But Jacob also left an opening in case his dream was nothing but a dream – he would not have to serve God. What are the operative words in Jacob's covenant at Bethel (this is the name he gave to the place where he had the dream)? "If...then." If God does what I want, then I'll do what He wants. The flip side, of course, says that if God doesn't do what I want, then I only have my own will to worry about. Jacob's covenant was with himself.

Jacob perfectly illustrates the person who comes into the church in order to make deals with God. "I'll pay a little attention, give a little money, spend a little time. But there'd better be a benefit, quick, quick, quick!" This is the person who is seeking a relationship with God rather than God Himself. This is the person for whom meditation on the subject of Christianity and pleasure is a very simple matter. A list of requests for Santa. The answer to the question, "what do I want," comes easily to this kind of Christian.

This could have been Jacob for the rest of Jacob's story, except that something happened very different the next time he encountered God.

---

[13] Genesis 28:16b
[14] Genesis 28:20-21

When Jacob met God next, he had amassed great fortune by shrewdly serving among his uncle's flocks. In fact, he amassed enough that the sons of his uncle grew jealous of him, and he found the same problem that he had when he lived at his own home - family members who wanted to kill him! The Lord spoke to Jacob and told him to go back home, but could he? What about his older brother, Esau? Wouldn't Esau still want to enact revenge for the stolen blessing?

As Jacob journeyed toward his brother, he became very concerned for the loss of property and life that he thought he might encounter. This is an important part of Jacob's story. When you don't own much, you don't care if you lose what you have. But when you own great assets and wealth, you become attached to the world and experience the attending anxiety. Jacob needed to hear from God before he would leave his uncle, and as he became more anxious during the journey, he reminded God that he was obeying the voice of an angel by traveling in the first place, "O God of my father Abraham and God of my father Isaac, the Lord who said to me, 'Return to your country and to your family, and I will deal well with you': I am not worthy of the least of all the mercies and of all the truth which You have shown Your servant, for I crossed over this Jordan with my staff, and now I have become two companies. Deliver me, I pray, from the hand of my brother..."[15]

You can see how Jacob had become much more than a man who followed religious ritual for family and ethnic reasons. He listened to God and responded. He thanked God for all that he had. He realized it was not by his own efforts that he had become a rich man. And he asked for God's mercy, a sure sign of repentance, a sure sign that Jacob knew himself and knew God.

So why the change? How did Jacob change from being a functional atheist to becoming a knower of God? The answer to Jacob's change will help us answer our own question, "What do I want?"

---

[15] Genesis 32:9-11

First, Jacob had become a mature man. He understood responsibility. He understood that his actions had an impact on the lives of other people. We can see, then, why he divided his company into two parts, "If Esau comes to the one company and attacks it, then the other company which is left will escape."[16] Why didn't Jacob say, "send everyone ahead, and if Esau is in a killing mood, I'll have time to run for it." I'll tell you why – that's not what a responsible man would say. No, Jacob wanted to preserve as much life and property as possible, as a responsible and mature man would, and he made his plans accordingly. When he finally approached Esau for the moment of truth, he himself went ahead of everyone to bow down seven times as a way of appeasing the anger he thought his brother still carried.[17]

So with us. The process of maturity is nothing more than the process of understanding that the things you do impact the lives of other people. So when we ask, "What do I want," we can agree that a mature answer takes into consideration the lives of other people (more about this in the eighth chapter). It's not just for those who are married or are parents. A mature man understands that his life influences the lives of all those around him no matter what his family situation may be. Just look at how much certain bishops and monastics have changed the world.

Second, Jacob had become a rich man. He had a stake in this world. This is a complicated part of our meditation in regards to the issue of Christianity and pleasure, because there are many God-loving people who have lots of money, and for whom the commonly designated pleasures of life are possible. Jacob had assets, wives, children, servants, and so on. God gave them to him. God wanted him to have them. Therefore, to some degree, we can assume that God wanted him to enjoy certain pleasures of life. How did Jacob maintain a great love and knowledge of God in the midst of such wealth?

---

[16] Genesis 32:8
[17] Genesis 33:3

First, he saw himself as a leader whose decisions had a lasting impact. He assumed an attitude of leadership that took into account many generations that were yet to come.

Second, Jacob attributed all his wealth to God. It is the same with us. If you're reading this right now, you're wealthy. You may not feel wealthy, but if all the people in the world right now were ranked in order of wealth and quality of life, you'd be much closer to the top than you can imagine. Look at the example of Jacob! The leadership, the attention to eternity, the life of continual thanks to God no matter what the circumstances. Remember, he wasn't always like that – remember the covenant made at Bethel, the deal with God? When we read of Jacob's return to the land of his home, we see a very different person. A very different way of knowing and conversing with God. A very different sense of eternity. Thanksgiving, every moment of every day. Prayer. Sacrifice. Fear of God that comes from a genuine knowledge of God and knowledge of oneself.

Third, Jacob came to understand that the hand of God was guiding his life and he struggled with the process of turning over control to God. I'm referring to the story of Jacob wrestling with an angel in Genesis 32:24-30. What did the angel say when he gave Jacob his new name? "Your name shall no longer be called Jacob, but Israel; for you've struggled with God and with men, and have prevailed." In what way did Jacob prevail? It certainly cannot be said that he won the fight. He prevailed because neither one of the wrestlers pinned the other, but nor did either one surrender.

So with us. When we come to the question, "What do I want?" we find that answering it is just like a wrestling match. The match will wound us, exhaust us, and last throughout the night. But we can never surrender.

As we ask ourselves what we want out of life, we must take into account those characteristics of Jacob's life that made him a man that drew near to God, that made him a man that knew God as his highest desire. Maturity. A concern for the well being of others. Worldly assets, and continual thanksgiving, the continual recognition that anything we have has come to us by way of the mercies and blessings of God.

To those who believe that God can be sought outside the church, or outside the realm of religious rites of worship, look at what happened to Jacob next. After Jacob had re-settled in Edom, God called him again to move away from his home: "Then God said to Jacob, "Arise, to up to Bethel, and live there, and make and altar there to God, who appeared to you when you fled from your brother Esau."[18] You see what God called Jacob to do? Go back to the place where he encountered divinity before, when he didn't know how to respond. God wanted Jacob to return to the place of empty ritual and make the ritual live. God gave Jacob a second chance to get the work of worship right.

So with us. We cannot say that we want God above all things and not spend as much time as possible worshipping Him in the church. If you still feel like you don't want to be in church, that it's a burden to go there, then you're at the level of Jacob during his first visit to Bethel, when he named the place Bethel, when he saw the dream of the ladder to heaven. You have a connection to God, but you don't have the wherewithal to respond appropriately. Take a lesson from Jacob. Allow your relationship to God to mature by seeking him in the gift he has given you, the church, and thereby allow yourself to discover the pleasure of wanting Him above all things.

Now, imagine you're standing in church, seeking God. You look at the icons, listen to the music, and close your eyes, praying along with the priest. But in front of you stands an unusual person, another worshipper, with funny clothing, or he's old, he's not paying attention and perhaps you can even smell him over the incense. It reminds you of another person you knew like that – some other old man who smelled funny all the time – and your mind wanders toward those memories.

---

[18] Genesis 35:1

Or perhaps a child is crying, and you wonder how young parents can be so selfish, remaining in the church with a noisy kid. What are some other possibilities? Perhaps your mind can't get away from the funny noise you heard in your car on the way to church, and you're thinking about how much it might cost to fix it.

Within seconds, you've gone from doing what you want – that is – seeking God above all things, to judging the people around you and letting your mind wander.

It happens, doesn't it? So now that you've answered the question, "What do I want?" you need to concentrate your attention on the organ of your body that can most help you focus on what you want. Your brain, and the mind it contains. This is the subject of our next chapter.

Fr. David R. Smith

3

CRUCIFY YOUR MIND

*　　*　　*

When I ask the question "What do you want?" I hope by now you answer, "I want God." That seems like an easy answer - easier to say than to achieve. But we have to try - it's the only consistently good desire of this life. When we succeed in focusing our idea of "things that are desirable" on God, then our sense of what is pleasurable becomes holy - and indeed, helps us to further focus our desire on things that do indeed bring us the most lasting pleasure in life. But it's like anything, it takes practice.

Previously, we learned something about pleasure – that it is fed by desire. What, then, feeds desire? Meditation. Contemplation. These are works of the mind.

The Mind of St. Paul

St. Paul can teach us something about this. When St. Paul wrote to the Corinthians about his "thorn in the flesh," he gave us a process by which we could train our minds to desire God and His perfect will. St. Paul begins by identifying a problem, "a thorn in the flesh was given to me, a messenger of Satan to buffet me."[19] So first of all, St. Paul became aware that something stood in the way of his comfort and enjoyment of life. We all do the same thing - when my tooth hurts, I decide to make an appointment with the dentist, when my cell phone bill comes, I decide to use it less, or when I see someone else get a promotion I wanted, I decide to pursue more education. St. Paul identified his "thorn in the flesh" as that which was keeping him from pleasure and giving him pain.

Now if you're uncomfortable with the word "pleasure" in my analysis of St. Paul's motives – stick with me. He'll use the word himself in just a few verses.

St. Paul prayed to God about his problem. "Concerning this thing I pleaded with the Lord three times that it might depart from me."[20] Why did he do this? Why didn't he just go to a physician and find out what the matter was with him and get it fixed? I think there are two reasons. First, he may have already gone to physicians, and they could not help. This would mean that St. Paul prayed to God for a problem that he had already tried to solve himself. And couldn't. This in itself is a good lesson for us - when we can't quite tell which way the will of God directs us, we need to try different paths. Until we find the one that God wants.

Second, the Holy Spirit was very strong in St. Paul, and so he could tell that the illness that afflicted him was not just a minor issue that an herb or a poultice could resolve. He turned to God in prayer for an illness that the Holy Spirit had told him could not be resolved medically.

My two points seem mutually exclusive. It might sound like I'm saying that St. Paul tried different things because he didn't know what God wanted him to do, while at the same time he knew exactly what God's answer was to his problem. That's what I'm saying, but the two are not mutually exclusive. There have been many times in my own life when I

---

[19] II Corinthians 12:7
[20] II Corinthians 12:8

knew that God had called me to undergo a certain trial, or to endure a certain affliction. That doesn't mean I didn't try to get out of it. That doesn't mean I didn't try to avoid the suffering to which he was calling me. I do not suffer willingly, even when I think that God has called me to it. Or to put it another way, when I know in my heart that God has called me to a situation that I dislike, I want to try everything possible to make sure that I'm hearing the Holy Spirit correctly. If I find a way out, you would hear me say, "thanks to God."

This is an important lesson for us as we try and address the issue of Christianity and pleasure. There are issues affecting your life right now that stand in the way of your enjoyment of life. Health, vocation, family, money. First, you must address them in whatever way you can, including, but not limited to, prayer. It's difficult, I know!

Second, you must continually make yourself a vessel of the Holy Spirit. He'll teach you whatever you need to know about anything and everything affecting your life. As God's will becomes apparent to you, the Holy Spirit's comforting breeze cools and refreshes your soul. He prepares you for the struggle ahead. Your fasting and prayer, your attention to the scriptures and worship in the church form you into a fitting and open container into which God's Holy Spirit can flow.

Next, St. Paul listened to the answer God gave him, "And He said to me, 'My grace is sufficient for you, for My strength is made perfect in weakness.'" It's difficult to welcome an answer like this. I know that I myself have brought concerns and problems to God in prayer, and I've felt the Holy Spirit's voice telling me that God would not resolve the problem in the way I wanted. I'll be honest, it's frustrating. I could feel the two wills within me, my own and God's, and it took a great effort to get them to match. The key to this passage of scripture is that St. Paul gave his sense of what he wanted over to God. He knew what he wanted. He sought it on his own, and when that failed, he went to God in prayer. But he was willing to listen to the voice of God saying, "No" and change his notion of what he desired.

Our Lord Himself did the same thing when He prayed, "O My Father, if it is possible, let this cup pass from Me, nevertheless, not as I will but as You will."[21] Here we see our Lord and Savior Jesus Christ, aware of His human will, but deciding to do, not what His human will wished, but the will of the Father.

But back to St. Paul and his thorn in the flesh. When he heard the big "no" from God, did that mean that St. Paul would have to just grit his teeth and bear the affliction that God wanted him to have? Before you answer, listen to the next verse: "Therefore I take pleasure in infirmities..." The rest of the verse is good, but we only need the first six words - therefore I take pleasure in infirmities. Pleasure. When St. Paul heard what the will of God was for him, when he knew for certain God's answer to his question, he decided to take pleasure in God's will, even when it was different than his own.

So what do you want? If you want God, then you have to be prepared when God's will for you is drastically different than your own will. You have to do more than *take* pleasure in the will of God, you have to *make* pleasure of the will of God. The pleasure may not exist. It almost certainly will not exist! You have to make it, often out of nothing.

The Flesh

Again, that's much easier to say than to do. In fact, it's something we could hear every day of our lives and we would still, in our last moments, find it to be a struggle. How can we make pleasure in the will of God, even when no pleasure exists?

We'll go back to scripture for an answer. Let's take a look at the word "flesh."

If a child asked you what the word "flesh" meant, you'd probably point to your hand or arm and say something like, "It's another word for skin." The scripture does indeed

---

[21] Matthew 26:39

use the word in this way, as in, "See my hands and my feet, that it is I myself; touch me and see, for a spirit does not have flesh and bones as you see that I have."[22] Perhaps our Lord Himself pointed to his hand or arm while saying these words. Perhaps He even pinched a little skin between His fingers.

St. Paul uses the word "flesh" this way, but he sometimes added another component that brings a much deeper meaning. For St. Paul, "flesh" did not only denote the human form and life in this world, but also was the opposite of "Spirit," as in, "for the mind set on the flesh is death, but the mind set on the Spirit is life and peace, because the mind set on the flesh is hostile toward God; for it does not subject itself to the law of God, for it is not even able to do so; and those who are in the flesh cannot please God" (Romans 8:6-8). What did St. Paul just say? Didn't he say that those in the flesh cannot please God? Then certainly, he cannot be using the word "flesh" as "skin," or "human life in this world," because that would mean that no living human being can ever please God. Doesn't our worship and repentance please God? Of course it does, at least when real repentance precedes worship. Didn't the saints please God? Of course they did. So then what does the word "flesh" mean in these verses?

One way to see what "flesh" means is to look at what flesh does - it entraps the mind and destroys our relationship with God. When the mind focuses on the flesh, it brings about 1) death, 2) hostility toward God, and 3) inability to follow the law or will of God. "Flesh," then, describes an attitude in which the mind focuses on those things that keep it from knowing God, from feeding the spirit. On the one hand, we become vessels for the Holy Spirit by making ourselves open to continual communion with God, while on the other hand, we close ourselves to God. We place our minds on the things of the world, ignore God's call, starve our spiritual

---

[22] Luke 24:39

selves, and cause our pursuit of worldly pleasure to bring us nothing but grief.

Let me give an example. Imagine a college student, during his first extended time away from home, studying and working hard his first week of school. He thinks off and on during the week about how he's going to a party on the weekend, and he wants to get really drunk. Stoned, smashed, wasted, whatever. His friends talk about the party, and he thinks about it more and more as the day draws closer. Now, let's say this college student has grown up in the church, and he can hear little voices in the back of his head, his parents and God, telling him that he shouldn't go to that party – or at least he shouldn't drink. At first, he pays attention to the voices, and determines not to overdo it. But the voices get quieter and quieter as he focuses his mind more and more on the party. Finally, when it comes to the moment of truth, his meditation on the things of this world have completely silenced whatever good counsel the voices of his parents and God had given. St. Paul describes it perfectly when he says this person "is not even able"[23] to overcome his fleshly inclinations, because he has completely squelched any influence his spiritual inclinations may have had.

This is one example, but the process happens all the time. In fact, the process happens in some people so often that the spiritual inclination is completely neutralized and those people do not have to think at all before committing sin. They are not tempted to sin because no temptation is needed. The person is totally obedient to sin, and has ceased to allow any struggle between the fleshly and the spiritual inclinations.

I remember sitting at a coffee hour after church one Sunday when an older member of our parish started to tell me something about someone. I asked her, "Is this gossip?"

She smiled. "Well, yes, Father, I suppose..."

"Then don't continue. I don't want to hear it," I said.

---

[23] Romans 8:7

She sat silently for a moment, but then started to tell me to story again.

Again, I told her to stop. "But I'm just saying, Father ..." she said. And before I could tell her to stop again, speaking very quickly, she revealed the entire story.

In this case, gossip was this woman's passion. She wouldn't have identified it as a problem – but that's one of the characteristics of a passion. The addict doesn't know she's an addict. The most obvious characteristic was that she simply couldn't stop. She could in no way prevent herself from revealing the gossip that she possessed. Even to a priest, even when the priest identified the talk as gossip, even when he told her to stop, she could not stop. The sin controlled her completely.

This illustrates the use of the word "flesh" in St. Paul. When you keep your mind focused on the things of the flesh, you become enslaved to the things of this world. In time, even when you want to change, to avoid doing things that destroy your life and your soul, you have no more choice in the matter. You have no choice but to continue: "For the flesh lusts against the Spirit, and the Spirit against the flesh; and these are contrary to one another, so that you do not do the things that you wish."[24] Again, St. Paul reveals this phenomenon, that a man can know what is the right thing to do, want to do it, and end up doing just the opposite.

The good news is that it also flows the other direction as well. You can see the works of the flesh, know that you desire them, and also see the will of God and know that you also desire that - and by simply making those distinctions, you can create desire where no desire existed and starve the flesh. You can reinvigorate your spirit and pull those desires that lead to destruction into the light. It really is miraculous. God will replace your evil desires with good: "I will give you a new heart and put a new spirit within you; I will take the heart of stone out of your flesh and give you a heart of flesh. I will put My Spirit within you and cause you

---

[24] Galatians 5:17

to walk in My statues, and you will keep My judgments and do them."[25]

Crucify Your Mind

You bring this about, feeding your spirit and starving your flesh (when "flesh" means a selfish attitude that destroys your soul), by carefully deciding where you put your senses. In the example above, my college student thought about his upcoming party all week long. He discussed it with his friends. Perhaps he even dreamt about it! Consequently, his senses sculpted the shape of his soul, and that shape threw him toward sin as soon as the opportunity presented itself. He filled his mind with images of sin, and thus he damaged his spirit.

But how can you not fill your mind with images of sin? How can you not allow the flesh to mislead you constantly toward those things that destroy the soul? Only one way: Crucify your mind.

Crucify. Put on the cross, sacrifice, take life away from, humiliate. This is what it means to crucify. Nail. Kill slowly. Lift up. Stretch. This is how we crucify our minds. Crucify your mind. It means put your mind on the cross. I'm not talking about simply thinking about the cross often. You've already heard a hundred sermons telling to you do this, and you still haven't started. No, I mean that you must decide that your mind is no longer your own. For instance, right now you're allowing my thoughts to occupy your attention. I'm writing this sitting at my desk in my study at church, and if I want to, I can draw your attention to any of the various things sitting on my desk (provided you continue reading). That's a high degree of control. In a way, when you read any book, your mind is not longer your own. But what happens when you stop reading, or I stop writing? Our minds begin to wander, because nothing controls them. They reassert their independence.

---

[25] Ezekiel 26:36

If the church decided that "preventing our minds from wandering" would become a spiritual discipline (complete with some attachment to the hours of the day or the calendar), it would most certainly be one of the easiest. When your mind is wandering, you can make it stop with no effort at all. Sometimes when I'm praying and my mind begins to wander, I shake my head back and forth a few times, and my mind re-focuses. What could be easier?

However, although it's easy to focus our minds for a moment, it's difficult to do consistently. It's difficult to give your mind to God, and not take it back a hundred times each day, putting it places God does not want it to be. Dreaming of luxury. Worrying about the future. Remembering wrongs. Judging others. Sometimes you find yourself doing these things, and you decide to stop. It's almost like waking up, like coming back to your senses. In fact, it's very, very much like coming back to your senses. When you force your mind to stop wandering, and put it on the things of God, your life goes back to making sense. Otherwise, it makes no sense at all.

Crucify your mind means: sacrifice it. When we spend all our time only thinking about the things that please us, and no time steering our minds toward God Himself, we go to bed anxious and dissatisfied. But when we desire a sense of inner peace, and seek it by sacrificing our minds, we soon find exactly what we've been looking for. When you sacrifice something, you give it up for a higher good.

At one point in my life, I had to spend time occasionally with a person who had wronged me many times. She had lied to me, cheated me, and constantly talked about me behind my back. When I tried to talk to her about it, she denied everything and acted as if we were the best of friends. I found that I was spending way too much time thinking about all the ways that she had wronged me, especially in the moments just before I knew I would have to see her. It was almost as if I was reminding myself of all the wrongs she had committed so that I could build up my guard against her when we had any contact. A natural human response, I suppose. It took great energy for me to stop doing this, and instead to focus my mind on God. I didn't force myself to forgive her, and I didn't think about ways I could make the situation better. I just prayed, and led my mind back again and again toward God. As a result, I felt nothing toward this person. I treated her, each time I saw her, as if I had no history with her at all. I let her continue to do bad things to me. And yes, she certainly kept doing them! Crucifying your mind is not a technique to get people to act nicely toward you. It's not a technique to resolve all your difficult relationships. In fact, it may not change any aspect of your outward situation at all. Crucifying your mind influences your inward situation.

Crucify your mind means: take away life from it. Active imaginations are for children! Once many years ago I put a new roof on our house. As I was working on a part of the porch outside my daughter's window, I heard her yelling and sounding very angry. I looked inside to see her sitting in the middle of all her stuffed animals. They had apparently been fighting among themselves, and she was scolding them. I spent some time sitting outside her window watching her interact with her toys. What a pleasurable break from roofing!

But what if you saw an adult doing that? You'd think the person should see a doctor, right? And yet, we all do this on occasion – daydream in ways that can only be described as fantasizing. Some might refer to this as having an "active imagination." It means that we allow our minds to graze in the fields of sin.

And that's exactly what our minds want to do – graze all the time. My wife tells me it's just because I'm getting old and grumpy, but I've started to notice drivers who don't go when a red light turns green. Often, when I'm stopped at a red light, I can see that the drivers in front of me aren't watching the light – they're doing other things: reading, talking on phones, playing with hair, makeup, coffee, or food. It's almost like they can't wait, they can't allow their minds to just sit still until the light changes. Then when the light turns green, they don't go because they don't see it. I'm not a horn blower by nature, but as I have noticed this phenomenon more, I've become one.

Can your mind stop wandering? Can it stop requiring that every minute be filled with restlessness? Can you eat alone without reading something or watching TV? Can you drive you car without the radio on? Can you wait for anything without becoming, sooner or later, fed up?

Crucify your mind. Cut off the wandering it so dearly wants to do. Let God become the life of your mind, and rest in Him.

Crucify your mind means: humiliate it. Romans designed the sentence of crucifixion in order to show their superior strength and domination. Crucifixion was not only painful, but humiliating. If you want to crucify your mind, you must embrace humility.

This is difficult. I remember a time in my life when I wanted to become more humble, and I prayed that others would get credit for the good things I had accomplished in my ministry (I was a camp director at the time). Guess what. God answered my prayers. My supervisor showed up one day to make a big deal about a member of my staff - how his ideas had made the summer the greatest ever. My first reaction was to scold myself for praying that prayer. It was clearly a prayer for someone more spiritually mature than me! My second reaction? I couldn't help but to tell the supervisor privately that many of the innovations were my ideas. I also told him that I felt good that someone else had gotten the credit - compounding my original pride with a false humility grown in a garden of even more pride. What a spiritual train wreck I often am!

This comes from self-love. When we truly and deliberately love God, we can see humility in the distance and even perhaps approach it. What did our Lord reveal as the greatest commandment? "You shall love the Lord you God with all your heart, with all your soul, and with all your mind."[26] The crucifixion of the mind begins in the love of God, which must supplant and destroy self-love.

$$*\qquad*\qquad*$$

So where have we come and where are we going? We've seen that one source of pleasure is desire, and so we've tried to answer the question, "What do you want?" After figuring out that the best answer to that question was, "I want God," we tried to find out how to desire God more than we do now. The answer? Crucify your mind. Give the workings of your mind over to God, and strive to let your thoughts rest in Him. What's next? More reflection on the mind – through encouragement to be thinkful in all things.

---

[26] Matthew 22:37

4

BE THINKFUL IN ALL THINGS

*   *   *

The chapter title is meant to be a play on words, not a mis-typing of the end of Colossians 3:15 ("be thankful"). No, I mean to say "be thinkful," and here's why: We've decided that we want God, and we can attain Him each moment of our lives by training our minds to focus on him continually. One way to do this is to "crucify your mind," but there is another way, and I call it "be thinkful in all things."

St. Maximos the Confessor described pleasure as "desire achieved," and desire as pleasure anticipated. If I desire to have something, say, a big screen TV, then I desire it because I expect that it will bring me pleasure when I own it. Desire is pleasure anticipated. But when I purchase the big screen TV, then I no longer desire it, because it's mine already, and I experience pleasure. Pleasure is desire fulfilled. Of course, my example is crude, but I use it to make a point. We all know that the pleasure one anticipates in owning a thing, when fulfilled, doesn't last very long. But it does in fact occur, even if only for the short time before we discover that the thing doesn't work like we thought it would or the credit card bill arrives, or we decide we want something else –

the fact that it occurs at all is what's important for my illustration.

People often cannot control the things they find pleasurable. Many people, in fact, gain pleasure from doing things that they do not want to do, like alcoholics, pedophiles, and arsonists - these are some extreme cases, but it applies just as well to gluttons, gossips, and exaggerators. How does the human mind work? How does it happen that we find ourselves gaining pleasure from something that we also are certain will bring us copious amounts of grief, pain, and regret? A man knows he will find only sorrow when he gives into temptation, and yet he surrenders to temptation regularly for the thrill he believes sin will bring! It's insane, quite literally.

But while we cannot control what we deem pleasurable, we can control what we deem desirable. Pleasure is uncontrollable. But desire we can handle. Remember what St. Maximos said? Pleasure is desire fulfilled. Controlling pleasure may elude us, but controlling desire is well within our power. How? Desire comes by way of meditation, planning, consideration, visualization, day-dreaming. Discussion. We can create desire within ourselves. We can create it by thinking constantly about the object of our desire. This is the whole foundation upon which the advertising industry is built. If an advertiser can get you to think about something long enough, and with good anticipation, then he's taken you a long way toward purchasing that product. That's why so much of advertising has nothing to do with the conveyance of information, but the nurturing of de-sire. Haven't we all seen TV commercials where you can't even tell what's being advertised until the very end – if then? Ask an advertiser. He will tell you that the commercial is designed to fill you with desire. He will tell you that desire is not a mysterious commodity at all, that it is very controllable. Pleasure is different. Advertising has nothing to do with pleasure. It's all about desire.

Our desires urge us to believe that something is going to bring us pleasure, but desire does not remain constant throughout our lives. The belief that certain things will give pleasure changes depending on what we contemplate at different stages of life. A young man may think that a nice car will bring him joy and fulfillment, but a more mature man realizes that the kind of joy the young man desires is not really available in a car. The pleasure one receives from a car is fleeting, at best. What's the difference? Experience. The experience of disappointment changes the framework of desire. The more mature man says to himself, "I remember expecting joy and fulfillment from owning a particular car, and when I owned it, the joy and fulfillment didn't come. So now that I'm older, when I go to buy a car, I desire different things than I did as a young man." Certainly maturity, not age, is the key here. The more mature man wants good value and reliability. The young man wants snazz. Desire changes as the man gets older, tempered by experience and previous disappointment.

See how it's a matter of control? The older man remembers his previous desires, he may even feel them now and again. But when he goes to purchase a car, he puts the immature desires away and decides to gain pleasure from a different kind of fulfilled desire. He uses his head. He thinks.

He thinks. We can choose where we put our minds, where we put our hearts, and thus we can control what we desire. How? The answer is easy. Contemplation and thought. The mechanism of controlling our desires is contemplation, the focusing of our thoughts. The mechanism to understanding desire, and thus to understanding pleasure, is contemplation, the focusing of our thoughts. St. Paul says it in his letter to the Philippians: "Be anxious for nothing, but in everything by prayer and supplication, with thanksgiving, let your requests be made known to God; and the peace of God, which surpasses all understanding, will guard your hearts and minds through Christ Jesus."[27]

In this beautiful passage of scripture, St. Paul first tells us not to be anxious – not to worry. I knew someone

---

[27] Philippians 4:6-7

who found a large amount of money in stock certificates in a box that she had inherited many years ago from a relative - over $300,000 worth. She put the stock into an account, but then immediately began to worry. I asked her to think about why she didn't worry about it in the past. After all, I reminded her, she went through the stock market crash (sorry, I mean "correction") of 1983 without one moment's worry! I showed her how she had lost thousands of dollars in value at that time, but hadn't lost one minute of sleep over it. Why start worrying now? Of course, the answer is simple. She didn't know she owned stock before she discovered the certificates, and so didn't worry about the market. But when stock ownership entered her consciousness, she watched the stock quotes on TV all day and worried when any little downward movement occurred. She started thinking about the market constantly.

Be anxious in nothing, says St. Paul. When you have something valuable, you think about it and worry about it. Is it possible not to do this? Can we own things that are valuable and not find ourselves worrying about them all the time? Sure, at least St. Paul gives us a plan by which we can try: "But in everything by prayer and supplication let your requests be made known to God." The greatest weapon in our arsenal. Prayer! If we ask God to help us and preserve us, watch out for us and protect us, then we rest in knowing that He has received our requests, and we know that whatever comes our way comes, at least to some degree, according to His will.

I say, "at least to some degree" because things happen to us sometimes that are not directly the will of God. God does not will tragedy into our lives. When I pray that my children would be safe and happy, it is not God's will to deny my request. However, there may be times when God uses tragedy for a further expression of His will, an expression of His will that I cannot see and do not understand. This is the secret to giving thanks for all things, as St. Paul tells us in another place: "In everything give thanks, for this is the will of

God in Christ Jesus for you."[28] When I love God, I turn over everything in my life to His will, and let Him decide what prayers are answered "yes" and what prayers are answered "no."

I may not like the answer I receive. But if an angel appeared to me and said, "whatever you are sorry or angry about right now – whatever you think is some kind of cosmic mistake – believe me, it's a part of the will of God," I would have to change my attitude. Why oppose the will of God? Will my life be better if I do? If I've given my life to God, and told him that I submit myself to him, does that only apply when I get the things I want? Clearly not!

Let me use this example: I have known nursing home residents that begin to curse loudly and use profanity as they age. Often, these are the last people you would expect would do this kind of thing. But what has happened? Perhaps throughout their lives they avoided giving thanks in all things and instead cursed under their breath when things didn't go their way. Then, when a touch of dementia enters the picture, the words spoken under the breath, which betray the opposite of the attitude that St. Paul is recommending, become loud and uncensored. Their newfound attitude surprises everyone around them, most of all the people who have known them for years as quiet and pious Christians. But is it such a surprise that this person is using foul language? He's angry, and for good reason: uprooted from home, cared for by strangers, poked at when he wants to be left alone and sometimes ignored when he would like assistance – "giving thanks in all circumstances" becomes a challenge that you and I cannot imagine. But what a surprise that the attitude of un-thankfulness that this person nurtured during the less difficult parts of his life has yielded an unexpected fruit: old age profanity.

Of course, this is not the reason St. Paul tells us to give thanks in all things, so that we would avoid becoming dirty old men and women. St. Paul knows that you're happiest

---

[28] I Thessalonians 5:18

when you give thanks, when you're putting your mind on good things. After all, how many of us give thanks after we've fallen into sin? "O God, thanks for letting me gossip about my friend today," or, "O Lord, thanks for the miserable attitude I had today which made me hurt the people I love." Does anyone say that? Of course not! You give thanks for good things, for children, for joy and success of those you love, for defeating the temptations of sin, for happy celebrations. These are the things for which we give thanks, and that's why St. Paul wants you to continually give thanks. Blessing from God are falling upon you every moment of every day, even when you think things are at their worst! By giving thanks, you recognize those blessings. Giving thanks in all circumstances forces you to think about good things. You put your mind on good things, and desire good things. You use your head. You think.

Of course, you receive the things you desire, which is the very definition of pleasure. "Delight yourself also in the Lord, and He shall give you the desires of your heart."[29] Do you want a life of constant pleasure? Don't buy a fancy car or try the latest diet. Instead, seek God and give thanks in all things.

St. Paul gives advice about how to do this: "finally, brethren, whatever things are true, whatever things are noble, whatever things are just, whatever things are pure, whatever things are lovely, whatever things are of good report, if there is any virtue and if there is anything praiseworthy – meditate on these things."[30] Use your head. Think about good things.

Something used to happen to me most every day, and I didn't recognize it until I read St. John of the Ladder: "There is an evil spirit, called the forerunner, who assails us as soon as we awake from sleep."[31] Every morning, as soon as I would get out of bed, I would begin to remember ways that people had wronged me. Events from long ago would pop into my

---

[29] Psalm 37:4
[30] Philippians 4:8
[31] St. John Climacus, The Ladder of Divine Ascent (Boston, Holy Transfiguration Monastery, 1979), 177

mind almost magically, and I felt the anger towards the perpetrator of the wrong almost as if it had happened that very moment. I could almost see the people before me: a bully bothering me on the way home from school, a feminist supervisor that hated all men, and probably a dozen or so guys that have "fixed" cars I've owned. Others as well. They would appear in my mind as I shuffled towards the bathroom, inviting me to begin my day in a sea of anger and bitterness. Why do the demons do that? Do they think that sometime in the future I'll be able to act on a plan of revenge that I made one morning as I brushed my teeth? No. They know that I've already forgiven these people, and that the worst I would do to them if I ever saw them again would be to avoid them. Why, then? It's because the demons want you to think about evil things all day long, and they can get you started best by assailing you in the morning, before you have time to think. It's like every day you have to run a race, and demons get the best of you by putting you way behind before you even get started.

St. John of the Ladder gives us an idea for how to stop this from happening: "There is an evil spirit, called the forerunner, who assails us as soon as we awake from sleep and defiles our first thought. Devote the first-fruits of your day to the Lord, because the whole day will belong to whoever gets the first start. It is worth hearing what an expert told me: 'from my morning,' he said, 'I know the course of the whole day.'"[32]

Wow. Indeed. No wonder he's a saint. When we think upon things that are good, and lovely, and just, and right, even in the seconds as soon as we wake from sleep, we have a good chance of making the desires that we nurture during the day good desires, and righteous. What a wonderful thing! Our pleasure, then, is not to think about how much we hate the people who have wronged us, or to even pray for their destruction, but it becomes our pleasure to accept with joy the unerring will of God for our lives.

---

[32] Climacus, 177

Thinking and Contemplation

Now, focusing your mind is not that hard over the short term. It's like running, even people who haven't done it for many years can do it at least a little. The difficulty comes when you try to focus your mind over the long term. This, everyone has found who has serious tried to do it, is almost impossible. I call it "being thinkful." To crucify your mind, you give you mind to God. To be thinkful, you focus your mind to the things that are important in life. You take care to be attentive to everything around you. This is the easiest thing to do. You don't have to give up anything besides those things that are distasteful anyway – bitterness, daydreaming, remembering wrongs, lust, greed, etc. When you learn to control the mind, you focus on good things, and this gives you pleasure. In addition, when we obtain those good things, your pleasure is doubled!

So why is it so difficult to be thinkful? This is why: Satan knows that if he can get you to let your mind wander undisciplined, you're his. Sin is "step ten" in a ten step process, and the flabby mind is step one. Perhaps Satan can't get you to sin as much as he wants, but if he can get you to take step one, he knows that it's only a matter of time before you take step ten.

Iconostasis is a difficult but rewarding book by George Florensky.[33] You want a mind exercise? Read this book. Right in the introduction, Florensky lets you know that he wants you to develop, clear, and focus your mind:

> Anyone who does things carelessly also learns to talk carelessly. But careless, unclear, inexact talk drags into its carelessness and unclarity an idea. My very dear, dear children: don't let yourselves think carelessly. An idea is God's gift

---

[33] Pavel Florensky, Iconostasis, trans. Donald Sheehan and Olga Andrejev (New York, St. Vladimir's Seminary Press, 1996)

and it needs to be taken care of. To be clear in
one's ideas, and to be responsible for them, is a
token of spiritual freedom and intellectual joy.[34]

Notice that he starts addressing clarity of thought by
addressing clarity of speech. What a great insight! We can all
tell how our minds work by listening to how our mouths work
- or how they would work if we had the courage to say what
we're really thinking. Every sin you commit started as a
thought, even when you've given yourself over to a passion,
and no temptation precedes the sin. At one point it did, and it
can again. As soon as you begin to try and think clearly about
your life and your behavior, then you'll find yourself stopping
to think about many things that before you didn't think about
at all.

"To be clear in one's ideas is a token of spiritual
freedom and intellectual joy." You won't feel free at first,
because the task is very difficult. The mind strains against the
leash like a big dog lunging to chase a squirrel, and Florensky
bids you hold tight, lean back, plant your feet.

Be thinkful. Be thinkful in all things.

There is a story of a king whose son did not live up to
the standards of a crown prince. One day his father, very
frustrated with the young man, gave him a bowl full of oil. He
told his son to leave the castle and walk around the city on a
particular route, accompanied by a member of the royal
guard. If the prince spilled even one drop of the oil, the king
had instructed the guard to cut his head off immediately. The
young man nervously took the bowl and walked very slowly
and carefully through the city, followed by the guard with
sword at the ready. When the prince arrived back at the castle,
the king asked him about the festival that was taking place in
the city at the time. The young man said, "I didn't see or hear
anything around me, I had all of my concentration on the
bowl of oil." The king told his son that, during his walk

---

[34] Florensky, 4

around the city that day, he had experienced something of the focus and attentiveness needed to occupy the throne of that land.

So with us. We make our way through this world, and a multitude of meaningless distractions seek our attention. Do we give them our attention easily? Indeed, many distractions seek our attention, and we have to choose which are meaningless and which need to be addressed. It's the ones that are pleasurable that cause us problems, right? Because all pleasures have dangers, even the ones that seem inherently good. We have to be thinkful in all things in order to decide which is which.

Suppose a man decides to drink alcohol. There's nothing wrong with that, but it's like playing with fire. It's dangerous. It's like putting electricity in your house. Electricity might make good things happen, and you might convince yourself that you can't live without it, but if your house burns down and you get cooked like a hamburger, then what good was electricity to you?

But it's not just alcohol or electricity. Let's take fasting, a good spiritual discipline. What if you fast constantly? You'll die of malnutrition. You can read stories of this happening, stories in which misguided monks left their monasteries in order to live lives of asceticism, and they literally ended up starving themselves to death. I'll tell you, that's more discipline than I have – thank goodness!

Therefore, even when we define a good desire and good pleasure, we must also define the dangers. We must be thinkful in all things. Anything except God Himself is imperfect, and may ensnare our souls with evil. Love for our children, for our country, knowledge of scripture – how could these things possibly be evil? I'll tell you! When they separate us from God, when we make them the very definitions of pleasure, then they become evil and we lose the benefits they offer.

A monk one time told me to give thanks for every bite of food, and I jokingly said that if I did this it would take hours for me to finish dinner. He looked at me very seriously and said, "then you're eating too much." He was right. Double. It is a wonderful spiritual experience to give thanks to God for every bite of food taken, and it certainly cuts down the amount of food that I eat.

When I give thanks to God for the things I have been given, I reckon their worth in terms of my relationship to God. "There are two means by which we can acquire such clarity of mind: the first and most necessary is prayer, by which we must implore the Holy Spirit to pour out His divine light into our hearts."[35] Prayer is a discipline of the church that focuses and heals the mind. It forces me to think about my life, about the passions that pursue me. All the disciples of the church provide me with a way to keep a suspicious eye always on those things that would ensnare my soul. Fasting makes me think about food, icons make me think about where I'm putting my eyes, the scriptures call me to ever-deeper levels of commitment to Christ. Be thinkful. "The second method of exercising the mind is always to examine things and probe deep for knowledge of them, in order to see clearly which of them are good and which bad." (Kadloubovsky and Palmer 1952, 90)

In the long run, everything I've said can be summed up in the five words, "be thinkful in all things." Your mind belongs to God, give it back to Him.

*   *   *

We're done looking at the first definition of pleasure: "Pleasure is desire fulfilled", and have learned that the key to controlling our own ideas of pleasure is to control our desires – by crucifying our minds and being thinkful in all things.

Now onto the second definition of pleasure: "Pleasure is that moment at which you might say, 'I wish this moment would last forever.'" Can this way of looking at pleasure offer the pious Christians any more insight into

---

[35] Scupoli, 90

having our ideas of pleasure help us, rather than hinder us, in our relationship with God?

5

SOMETIMES PLEASURE IS THE OPPOSITE OF PAIN

*   *   *

If pleasure is that moment at which we say "I wish this moment would last forever" (my second definition from chapter one), then we can define "pain" as the moment at which we say, "I wish this could be over quickly." In this way, the opposite of pleasure is pain - but only when I define pain very broadly. I'm not limiting the word "pain" to the alarming sensation that tells living things they're in distress. Rather, for this discussion, I define pain as anything one wishes not to prolong. In this way, it can be a form of pain to drive to the grocery store. At least, it is if you're in a hurry and want to get your grocery shopping done as quickly as possible. Or if your car doesn't work right and driving it makes you stressed. Or everyone at the grocery store speaks a language you don't know and don't want to learn.

On the other hand, driving to the store is not painful if you love driving your car, or if the only time during the day you find peace and quiet is when you're running errands.

When we define pain and pleasure very broadly, they overlap one another. Pain becomes pleasure, which becomes pain again. Let me show you how.

Throughout high school, and for two years of college, I played the violin with the goal of becoming a professional musician. At that time, whenever I heard great violinists play, their music inspired me, and I ran home to practice and practice in order to play like them. Unfortunately, I really started to get serious about the violin too late in life, and I couldn't catch up to others who had started music lessons before they started eating solid food. But I tried. I stayed in my room nights and weekends practicing. I worked to save money to get better and better instruments and pay for expensive lessons and camps.

Practicing was a pain. But I loved it. During my classes at school I thought only about the violin, and I hurried home so I could start practicing. But how could that be? How could it be that something as difficult, frustrating, and time-consuming as learning the violin could be something I longed to do more than anything else? It had to do with my perception of pleasure. I knew that if I practiced hard, I would gain pleasure from the violin, and if I didn't, I wouldn't. So when I practiced, I pre-felt the pleasure of playing well. I welcomed the feeling of success and musical accomplishment that I could see off in the future by applying that anticipated pleasure to present pain.

So pain became pleasure, which, as I increased my expectations of myself as a musician, became pain again. Then pleasure. Many people do this. They learn to enjoy certain kinds of pain because it points to a pleasure they wish to experience – hunger pain leading to a slender physique, physical exertion to good health, spiritual ascesis to a greater communion with God in Jesus Christ, and so on. These pains are linked to the anticipated pleasures such that they become pleasures in themselves.

But how does this happen, spiritually speaking? How can we learn to link anticipated pleasure to present pain in order to draw closer to God? How do we employ this phenomenon of pleasure and pain to achieve spiritual goals?

The fact is that people can choose pain. Humans have the ability to embrace pain, even re-define it as pleasure, in the interests of achieving something they want. Sometimes that something is a noble goal, and other times we simply want to avoid trouble and annoyance. But the seeking of the higher pleasures that distinguish us from animals is a possibility for all men. My wife and I jokingly say of our dogs, "They have no morals." Of course they don't. They're dogs. If no one is watching them, they eat the cat's food, and if he complains, they bite him. But when someone's home, both dogs steer clear of the cat's food and generally ignore him. Why? To avoid punishment. That's their only motivation. They care nothing for postponing pleasure. A dog does pretty much want it wants to do all the time, within the strictures reality has placed on it. If my dog could fly through the air and catch squirrels, he would. Even if he wasn't hungry. Even if he wasn't cold. But people can choose pain. We can give meaning to pain. We can even enjoy pain when we know it's leading to something we like. How?

Choosing Pain

First, we must crucify our minds, and be thinkful in all things, but you already know that. These are ways of saying that we must focus our minds on God. When God occupies our thoughts, pain and discomfort become bearable and even, in a way, pleasurable.

Second, we must meditate upon the anticipated pleasure, the end of all pain. Heaven. We must understand heaven, study it, believe in it, think about it. Read about it. There are two places in the gospels that teach us about the anticipation of heaven. As our Lord Jesus hung dying on the cross, one of the criminals hanging nearby asked for salvation and received it. "Then he said to Jesus, 'Lord, remember me when You come into Your kingdom.' And Jesus said to him, 'Assuredly, I say to you, today you will be with Me in

Paradise."[36] Aha. Now we've learned one thing about heaven – Jesus refers to it as "paradise." We also know beyond any doubt that the criminal on the cross dwells in heaven right now, because Jesus promised him he would.

But let's look further. The physical suffering of the "good thief" did not stop when Christ saved his soul. Our Lord drew that man's attention to the comforts that awaited him in the heavenly kingdom, where sickness, sorrow, and sighing have all fled away. But that man didn't miraculously disappear from the cross, to find himself sitting in front of a good meal in a distant city. Nor did he instantly die. But do you think he found his sufferings more bearable because of what Jesus had said to him? Absolutely!

So with us. When we hear the words of Christ telling us that He has called us to the particular circumstances under which we suffer, and that the suffering of this world cannot compare to the joys of Paradise, we gain hope. Hope that strengthens and encourages. Hope that gives understanding, endurance, and forgiveness. Hope that calms our minds as we wait for the time when God calls us either home to Himself or on to other circumstances.

We also learn about heaven another place in the gospels, when Jesus was teaching the disciples privately. St. Peter asked a question that he would not have asked in public: "See, we have left all and followed You. Therefore what shall we have?"[37] This is certainly an honest question coming from a practical, self-employed man. What's my return on this investment?

One might expect Jesus to tell St. Peter that he already had his reward – the truth of God. Salvation. Forgiveness of sins. Mercy. But no, Jesus forms an answer with the same practicality that delivered the question: "Assuredly I say to you, that in the regeneration, when the Son of Man sits on the throne of His glory, you who have followed Me will also sit on twelve thrones, judging the twelve tribes of

---

[36] Luke 23:42-43
[37] Matthew 19:27

Israel. And everyone who has left houses or brothers or sisters or father or mother or wife or children or lands, for My name's sake, shall receive a hundredfold, and inherit eternal life."[38] This is not an "it's not about material things" answer. Jesus tells St. Peter that giving up earthly joys will result in heavenly joys a hundred times better. Eternally!

This passage plainly says: embrace the short suffering of this world, and you'll gain the eternal rewards of the next.

Third, we must identify every moment of our suffering on earth as an offering, a co-suffering, with God. God forgives sin by absorbing the results of sin, suffering and death, into Himself. This is why Christ came to this world to suffer. God gives us the opportunity, insofar as we desire to become Christlike, to join Him in His suffering for the world. We do not fill anything lacking in His suffering when we suffer with Him, but rather we become "little Christs," preaching to the world the good news of the gospel of salvation by showing the meaning of Christ's incarnation. He forgave sin by suffering. What better way of living that message than by becoming a co-sufferer with Him?

The Eucharist brings this point home each time we prepare ourselves to partake. Suffering fills the Eucharist, which in turn fills us. When the priest indicates the bread on the paten, he says, "Take, eat, this is My Body, which is broken for you for the remission of sins." It's broken. It's the body of Christ. What could express suffering any more strongly than that? The wine in the chalice, "Drink ye all of this: this is my Blood of the New Testament, which is shed for you and for many, for the remission of sins." Again, it's shed, and it's the blood of Christ. There is no shed blood without suffering.

The next time you take Holy Communion, fix your mind on how much you're embracing and agreeing to embrace Christ-like suffering for the world.

---

[38] Matthew 19:28-29

The Pain We Do Not Choose

I say that we must learn to choose pain, because choosing pain gives meaning to our suffering and to our lives. But there is another kind of pain, the pain that we do not choose. I mean sickness, or the suffering of those we love, or long term sufferings like poverty and family problems. These kinds of pain we do not choose, we do not wish them upon ourselves. They are different than fasting or vigils or prayers, where we choose the length and severity of the pain, and more easily give the suffering to God. If we don't want the pain, and try everything possible to get rid of it, how can we count ourselves co-sufferers with Christ?

It's not one or the other. At creation, there was no pleasure or pain. There was only an unending communion with God and enjoyment of His creation. But man turned his attention to what he could not have, the most amazing yet predictable decision in human history. I mean, if you could have everything and live in a garden paradise, why in the world would you want to eat the one piece of fruit that would ruin the whole deal? It's because this is the nature of men. When my children were little, I could put them in a room full of toys and point out the one thing - the telephone, a lamp, the computer - that they were not allowed to touch, and guess where they would go first. You know the answer! It's the same thing in the scriptures. You and I would define the Garden of Eden as nothing but pleasure, but Adam and Eve illustrate how desire is linked to pleasure. When God pointed out the one thing they could not touch, desire was born. Could they really be content knowing that one desire remained out of their reach? Remember what the snake said to Eve, "For God knows that in the day you eat of it, your eyes will be opened, and you will be like God, knowing good and evil."[39] What part of this is a lie? None of it. Satan stirred up desire in Adam and Eve by stirring up curiosity, and

---

[39] Genesis 3:5

tapping into the tendency all men have to seek change just for the sake of change.

Man turned his attention away from God, and began to desire other things. This began the reign of death. Anything that draws us away from God brings about death in our souls, perhaps not immediately, but eventually. It's like smoking. When you smoke your first cigarette, you don't die. You don't even have trouble breathing, at least when you're done. So you can smoke a pack, two packs, a carton, two cartons. In a way, each cigarette contributes to your death, although you certainly can't feel any difference from one cigarette to the next. Or perhaps even one year to the next. But it happens, slowly but surely. Just because it happens slowly doesn't mean it's not happening surely. It's the same with sin, it often happens without our knowledge, and creeps up on us slowly. What can God do to bring us back to Himself? How can He keep us from spending day after day rejecting Him, knowing better than we do how we're marching step by step toward an eternity in hell? How we don't seem to realize it, because it happens very slowly, but it still happens nonetheless?

Pain. That's the answer. Pain. Pain is sometimes a gift of God that sounds the alarm and tells you you're going in the wrong direction. Pain.

Pain is the opposite of pleasure, and sometimes it's a gift of God. Why would a man change when he's experiencing pleasure upon pleasure? How would a man feel sorry for his sin if he never feels sorrowful at all? He wouldn't. Without the pain that brings us back to God, we continue to forsake His truth. Pain brings us back to God, back to life. Desire for anything other than God leads to death, and pain is the alarm that tells us that we are wanting the wrong things. Pain is the smoker's cough that says it's time to quit.

St. Maximos the Confessor commented on this kind of pain: "Because of the meaningless pleasure which invaded human nature, a purposive pain, in the form of multiple sufferings, also gained entrance."[40] God keeps us from meaningless pleasure, which will destroy our souls, by sending us pain.

Not all suffering is given by God. Not all pain comes from God. God may have ordained pain as a part of creation, but He does not ordain all the pain that human beings experience. In other words, we cannot always see a direct correlation between sin and punishment. A drunk driver may throw up in his car and smash it into a tree, but does that exhaust the pain his sin has caused? Not at all. His family suffers, the community suffers. The guy who owned the tree suffers. His son suffers, growing up with this sin of his alcoholic father. The boy's future family and co-workers suffer. You do not experience all the pain that your sins cause. Other people experience it as well - often undeserved, at least in terms of particular sins and particular punishments. I say "particular punishments" because everyone deserves all suffering, because everyone sins continually, forsaking the law of life. But some who sin little suffer much, and some who sin like the devil don't seem to suffer at all. The results of your sins will even outlive you! It's not just widespread, it's long-term!

Perhaps at some point in the judgment we'll be able to see the ripples our sins have caused, reaching out to all the world and throughout generations. Creating death, the ultimate pain. In it, we lose everyone and everything we have. But where does it have its origin? In the pain that we make necessary by longing for something other than God! As I said before, it's quite literally insane, that men would choose death over God. But we do, all of us.

The key for our present discussion is to turn the pain that brings us back to God into pleasure, so that we would understand and embrace the reason God created it in the first place. To say, no matter what, "I deserve this." To say, no matter what happens to you, "I deserve this."

[40] St. Nicodemos of the Holy Mountain and St. Makarios of Corinth, The Philokalia: The Complete Text (Volume 2). Edited and Translated by G.E.H. Palmer, Philip Sherrard and Kallistos Ware (London, Faber and Faber, Ltd. 1981), 244

Of course, you may say to me, "But I don't deserve all the things that have happened to me." Let's say, for the sake of discussion, that's true. Perhaps you don't. But I'm not talking about justice here, I'm not talking about your guilt or innocence, I'm talking about a way of perceiving pain and pleasure that will draw us close to God.

Again, St. Maximos contributes to the discussion:

> "Once human nature had submitted to the syndrome of pleasure freely chosen followed by pain imposed against one's will, it would have been completely impossible for it to be restored to its original life had the Creator not become man and accepted by His own free choice the pain intended as a chastisement for man's freely chosen pleasure."[41]

In other words, Jesus our Lord breaks the cycle of seeking pleasure and experiencing pain. He took into himself the penalty we suffer for neglecting God. He, more than any man who has ever lived, did not deserve the pain He suffered. But He accepted it, embraced it. He walked along a pathway of suffering for the redemption of the world, leaving a path by which we also can become Christ-like by following it, step by step.

You don't have to stop praying for relief from your pain in order to give your suffering to God, not at all. Nor should you reflect on the sufferings of Christ as a source of guilt, or a debt that you owe. You continue to pray that God would deliver you from your illness or circumstances, but if the answer is "no," you respond by giving thanks, and rejoice in God's mercy.

Training for Repentance

Before we leave the issue of pain, let's look at one more

---

[41] St. Nicodemus, 244

characteristic of pain freely chosen - the training of ourselves for repentance. Even though God has given us a way to overcome the cycle of death, we still continue to choose death over life. Why? It's simple: when I am born again to a new life in Jesus Christ, my soul is enlightened but my nature does not change. I'm still a sinful human being, living in a fallen world. We've seen in our discussion of Christianity and pleasure how we find ourselves wanting one thing and doing something different. God has written His law in your heart, so you know right from wrong, but you still choose the wrong.

Forgiveness brings us back when we fall away, but what about the frustration we feel of continually falling into sins and not recognizing it until after it's happened? This brings us to the spiritual discipline of choosing pain. When I impose upon my body some kind of pain, I remind it that my mind will not relinquish control, that my mind wants to obey God in all things. The body cries out, but the mind is greater. Again, I'm defining pain broadly – I don't mean that we should cut ourselves with knives as a spiritual discipline, but that we should embrace training in Christ-likeness, aim for the opposite of pleasure, agree to spend time doing something about which people normally say, "I wish this could be over quickly." Fasting is an example. When I introduce the discipline of fasting to people who haven't tried it before, they often comment about the intricacies of the calendar and the foods forbidden and allowed. And while we must learn and practice these intricacies, they do not contain within them the real purpose of fasting. I'm not holier simply by refusing the omelet in March that I ate in January. I become holier when I use fasting to progress toward a greater communion with God in Jesus Christ. When I choose pain.

In doing this, I recount the pain that Christ suffered for my sin. It's easy to make the connection, too, because my body whines like a dog when it doesn't get what it wants. Like Wimpy in the old Popeye cartoons, it promises to gladly fast on Tuesday for a hamburger today. The extent to which my body rails against any self-imposed discipline, especially one spiritual in nature, brings me to a real, emotional connection with the necessity of pain as something that steers me back to God.

So pain is the opposite of pleasure, but it can become pleasure when we give it to God and recognize how it helps us grow in Christlikeness. "I wish this moment would last forever" becomes, "I wish this was over quickly, but if it's not, I'll use it as a way to draw closer to God."

What happens when we become impatient with the entire arrangement? When we decided that we've had enough of pain? In the next chapter we'll look at the fact that all suffering, although not all striving, will have an end. While we live in this world, we must constantly consider that it is not our home.

6

WE HAVE NO HOME IN THIS WORLD

*   *   *

Sometimes we might define pleasure as "I wish this moment would last forever." Pleasure is something you want to last. A place where one can dwell for awhile, relax, enjoy life. A home. Everyone wants a home.

That tendency, the longing we all have for a home, makes up a large part of our quest for pleasure. People make "home" in the most interesting places – school lockers, hospital rooms, office cubicles, the insides of cars. We all want our own space. There's nothing wrong with this - it certainly isn't the will of God that we all live in de-personalized environments. But we must balance this with the constant recollection that this world is not our home.

When a certain scribe said to Jesus that he wanted to become a disciple, Jesus told the man, "Foxes have holes and birds of the air have nests, but the Son of Man has no where to lay his head."[42] What did our Lord mean? The scriptures do not tell us much about this scribe, but we can tell something

---

[42] Matthew 8:20

about him from the way our Lord answered him. The scripture implies that the man decided not to follow Jesus, so the fact that the disciples of Jesus would have no homes must have been the factor that turned him away. Why? It's simple. He was probably like me and you - he valued his land, his home, his space. Perhaps his city, province, or country. "Are you ready to be a homeless missionary, and go to a strange place from which you will never return? And even there, have no space to call your own?" Jesus asked him. The man's answer was clear – "absolutely not."

If getting heavenly treasure means giving up one's earthly mite, many would decline the offer. Would you have? For me, when I was young, no. But as I get older, and I enjoy more and more a place to call my own, it's a harder question to answer. I find that as years go by I tend to seek more of my own space in this world. A home, land and property. I cannot say that I would have decided not to follow Jesus – I can't even imagine walking away from Him as that scribe probably did. But nor can I imagine giving up all my earthly possessions. Seriously. I guess I'm like Job in that way – if you took away my family, my home, all my belongings, and my health, I might be most inclined to take for myself "a potsherd with which to scrape" myself while I "sat in the midst of ashes."[43] I know that my wife would not urge me to "curse God and die," but I also know that the two of us would grieve long and hard together before we could decide what to do next.

Most North American Christians have a home in this world. In the same way that the church fathers urge you to meditate on your own death as a spiritual discipline, perhaps it's also a good discipline to meditate on the loss of your home and family. Can we do that? Isn't that a much more difficult thing to meditate on? I spoke to a man one time who had been in a car accident where his wife and one of his children were killed. He had been the driver and had fallen asleep. Afterwards, someone had said to him, "well, at least

---

[43] Job 2:8 (paraphrased)

you're alive," and he was very upset about it. He came to church to talk about it, and said to me, "I'd much rather be dead right now. There are many things in this world worse than being dead."

To this day, I weep when I recall him saying those words. But I agree with him. Meditating on my own death is much easier than meditating on the death of my family and the loss of my home.

What Does "Home" Mean?

As our Lord delivered His last long teaching to the disciples before His arrest and crucifixion, one of the disciples wondered how Jesus would manifest Himself to the disciples, but not to the world.[44] This disciple didn't grasp that Jesus would die, and thus not be seen anymore by the world, but would rise again, and thus manifest Himself to His followers. It didn't make sense – if Jesus had come to establish a world-wide kingdom, how could He do that and be invisible to the world?

Jesus answered the disciple, "If anyone loves Me, he will keep My word; and My Father will love him, and We will come to him and make Our home with him." Here our Lord defines the Christian concept of "home." It means communion with God, it means following the will of God in all things, it means loving God. "Home" in Christianity does not describe a place where you live and keep your stuff. St. Paul said it best, "While we are at home in the body we are absent from the Lord."[45] Of course, St. Paul speaks in this passage about the body, not about a physical dwelling that a person might purchase or rent. But St. Paul apparently never had a "home" in this manner of speaking – but if he had, don't you think that he'd have the same attitude about a physical home as he did about his physical body?

---

[44] John 14:22
[45] II Corinthians 5:6

For a time in my life, I worked to arrange adoptions of Guatemalan children from an Orthodox monastery /orphanage in Guatemala to North American families. I loved to go to Guatemala, especially after I'd visited several times and learned my way around a bit.

But it was very different when I went with my wife to pick up our own adopted daughter. Before that visit, I had always been confident – helping people through a process that I understood in a city that I could navigate. When it came to our own adoption, though, I was out of sorts somehow. I didn't know why. I felt nervous; I wanted everything to go perfectly. I suppose that a delay in someone else's adoption would not have irritated me nearly as much as a delay in my own.

The last step was to go to the US embassy to get our daughter's visa to travel into the United States. When we drove up to the building, we encountered a huge line of people, police everywhere, cars driving through the small space at high speeds, and tons of noise. An average day at the US embassy, but it still made me very worried. We stepped into a small line for Americans, and went through the gates very quickly. For the first time, I felt sorry for all the people waiting in the long lines in the hot sun. I wondered if they resented us at all – cutting ahead of the whole mess. Then we walked into the building. A guard spoke to us in English, and there were pictures of the president and the US Secretary of State in the entryway. I found myself breathing an almost involuntary and surprising sigh of relief. We went to wait in a comfortable air-conditioned room full of adoptive parents who all spoke English and shared very similar experiences with the Guatemalan adoption system. It felt so good, like everything would be fine. In a way, we had arrived home. In fact, I don't think I felt as much relief when we actually, a day later, stepped onto American soil in New York. Why?

Well, when you're "out of sorts," not feeling well, where do you want to go? Home. We all want to belong. We all want to be home. But there is no home in this world for the Christian. If the world has become our home, we absent ourselves from the Lord. The world cannot be our home, because doing the will of God is our home. A nation cannot be our home because loving God is our home, and our nationality.

At Home Without a Home

It's difficult to learn to be at peace in situations that remind us of the temporary character of life. In chapter one, I described trying to live like a monk during Lent one year, and how I longed to give up my deprivations when Pashca came. But monks don't do that! They don't start watching TV and listening to talk radio after Pascha – they continue with their "deprivations" – but how? They don't view the fast as a time of deprivation; they know it's a time of spiritual joy. They find pleasure in Lent, whereas I took pleasure in thinking about the end of Lent. I concentrated on the deprivation, they concentrate on the Lord. What made me feel most at home at that point in my life? Sitting on my couch surrounded by my family, watching TV and enjoying a little snack. But when does the monastic feel at home? With the Lord! The monastic, who owns nothing or very little, who enjoys the pleasures of family in a very different way than most people do, who rests in work and obedience and the pursuit of spiritual enlightenment – every day this man recalls the fact that this world is not his home, and establishes his home with the Lord even while living in this fallen world.

The life of a certain Athonite saint, St. Maximos Kavsokalybites, "the hut burner," has stirred me every since I heard of him. St. Maximos had a great devotion to the Theotokos, and gained great spiritual wisdom at an early age because of his prayers and attention to spiritual things. In order to mask his wisdom, he often feigned madness. After living on Mt. Athos for some time as a normal monk, he went into the wilderness, and after seeing a vision of the Mother of God telling him to live alone there, started his remarkable life of ascesis and love for God alone. He lived in small huts he built out of sticks and bark, but after a short time he would burn the hut and move to another place. Most of the monks on the holy mountain dismissed him as insane.

St. Gregory the Sinaite, a great teacher of the ascetic life, spent some hours talking with St. Maximos and learned much about the prayer of the heart from him. He urged St. Maximos to stop his ascesis of hut burning, and told him to settle in one place so that the other monks could benefit from his teaching. St. Maximos did this, and offered spiritual help to many monks, hierarchs, and two emperors. He is venerated on January 13th.

I think I admire this saint so much now partly because of the amused reaction I had when I first heard of his life. I feel bad for judging him in my mind – for asking (while laughing, I confess) the person I was with at the time what possible spiritual benefit there could be in building little huts and then burning them down.

But as I began to think more and more about St. Maximos, it occurred to me that he was really onto something. Now, tell my wife not to worry, I'm not going to burn our house down as a way of following the example of St. Maximos! But his example teaches me to walk into my house each day with the full knowledge that it is not mine. With the knowledge that my house is temporary, worldly, physical, a drain on resources, a humiliation to the poor, a receptacle for useless clutter. It takes my time. It contains my indolence. It hides my impiety. St. Maximos recognized this reality, the reality of the dwellings we make for ourselves while we live on earth. What valuable teaching! He didn't need to write anything – his teaching that "this world is not our home" whooshes and crackles through the almost seven centuries since his death, railing at us to stop worrying about what tomorrow will bring, because tomorrow has enough troubles of its own. St. Maximos Kavsokalybites, pray to God for us!

Peace

The urge to find a home in this world comes from a desire for rest and peace. This is probably why I didn't worry about a permanent home so much when I was younger – I had more than enough energy to maintain a kind of permanent restlessness. But at this present point in my life, I could more often than not use a little rest. It reminds me of one of the proverbs of Solomon: "A little sleep, a little slumber, a little folding of the hands to rest; so shall your poverty come like a prowler, and your need like an armed man."[46] See what Solomon is saying? The attitude that this world can be my home, a place of peace and rest, creates poverty. Spiritual poverty, I might add. But doesn't that sound good, at least sometimes? Not the poverty, but the little sleep, and little slumber? Many days, it sure does to me!

Well, at first it does. But when we seek after the peace that the world has to offer, we only compound our inner chaos. We all want peace. It sounds good. And we can have it – we just need to search for and work for the right kind of peace. Real peace, lasting peace, eternal peace. "These things I have spoken to you, that in Me you may have peace," Jesus said. "In the world you will have tribulation; but be of good cheer, I have overcome the world."[47]

Let's look at this passage for a moment. Why would anyone choose tribulation? If Christ offers us peace, why wouldn't everyone follow Him without question? I'll tell you why. It's because the tribulation that the world has to offer clothes itself in a mask of peace, a mask of peace that appears attractive to the sinful nature that continually controls us. This means that there are two kinds of peace – the real and the false. Even our Lord used the word in two different ways. In contrast to the passage from St. John's gospel I quoted above, Jesus also says that He does not come to bring peace. "Do not think that I came to bring peace on earth, I did not come to bring peace but a sword."[48]

Look at these two verses together. The Savior came to this world so that we would have peace, but He did not come to bring peace. How is this possible?

---

46 Proverbs 24:33-34
47 John 6:33
48 Matthew 10:34

First, in the passage from St. John's gospel, Jesus tells the disciples (and all who listen to His words in the generations after) that they (His words) will help them achieve peace. But what kind of peace? A nice quiet life in a big house? Not at all. Our Lord reminds us that the world will not become a peaceful place just because Christians have discovered inner peace. "In the world you will have tribulation." The world will remain chaotic, but it won't destroy you because you'll have inner peace. As Isaiah wrote: "'I create the fruit of the lips; Peace, peace to him who is far off and to him who is near,' say the Lord, 'and I will heal him.' But the wicked are like the troubled sea, when it cannot rest, whose waters cast up mire and dirt. 'There is no peace,' says my God, 'for the wicked.'"[49] Indeed. There is no peace for the wicked – and guess what? His lack of peace will have a sure influence on your life, perhaps will even end your life, but it cannot steal the genuine and lasting peace that God gives.

Look at how this works. There is no peace in this world, but Christians living in this world can, and do, find inner peace. Our peace is not connected to this world, nor is it contingent upon this world. It comes from God, as St. Paul reminds us: "For the kingdom of God is not eating and drinking, but righteousness and peace and joy in the Holy Spirit."[50] (Romans 14:17). Here, the great apostle tells us that we may not have joy in worldly terms, but that we can still enjoy the peace that comes from God, and find pleasure in it.

This is why our Lord says in St. Matthew's gospel that He did not come to bring peace. This world will never be characterized by harmony and love. Many will not seek the peace that God brings, and in fact, their lack of spiritual peace and stability will, like a giant vacuum cleaner, suck Christians into conflicts that they have not devised and do not want.

Remember the first three petitions of the Great Ektenia in the Divine Liturgy. "In peace let us pray to the Lord" calls us to separate ourselves from the earthly cares that

---

wait for us outside the doors of the church, and to cast every bit of our attention and love on God. "For the peace from above and the salvation of our souls, let us pray to the Lord," implores us to pray that we would gain our sense of peace, rest, home "from above," not from below.

Then the liturgy speaks of the second kind of peace, the peace of this world. "For the peace of the whole world, the good estate of the holy churches of God, and for the union of all men, let us pray to the Lord," calls us to recognize that the peace of God is available to all men, regardless of place or time, and that we desire that all would know that peace. Of course, it won't happen. It can't happen. The entire world will never embrace God's peace, His holy and pleasurable will for their lives – but that doesn't stop us from praying for it.

I like to think of it this way. I'm standing on the deck of a ship and there are a thousand people drowning in the water. I know I can't save all of them, but I'm sure going to try. There will never be peace in this world, but Christians can never give up searching for it. As St. Peter tells us, "He who would love life and see good days, let him refrain his tongue from evil, and his lips from speaking deceit. Let him turn away from evil and do good; let him seek peace and pursue it."[51] We all want to love life and see good days, correct? St. Peter gives us advice that we all can follow; don't speak evil or lie, and turn away from evil. But he also gives us advice that we should pursue although it will never be achieved – "seek peace and pursue it."

I was at a conference of nursing home administrators recently and the moderator asked us what words come to mind when he said the word "home." I noticed that many of the words from the participants were contradictory – one man said "noisy" and another said "quiet." One said "peaceful," and another, "chaotic." One said, "wide open spaces" and another said, "a little place to call my own." In fact, for every

---

51 I Peter 3:10

description that someone suggested, one could say the opposite and it would apply.

I didn't offer my answer, because it would not have confused the participants and moderator, but the words "to know the will of God and do it" came to my mind.

7

HEAVEN BEGINS TODAY

*   *   *

Are you sure you're going to heaven when you die? I used to ask this question of people when I "did evangelism" as a Protestant pastor. I would ask people if they were going to heaven, and if they said yes, I would ask them why they thought so. People gave the wrong answers almost all the time, and my evangelism consisted of teaching them the right answers. It was all very intellectual, and if the person decided to become a Christian, the prayer we prayed was very clinical.

But now I think I was asking the wrong questions. At that time, I thought that Christians should know, should have an absolute assurance, that heaven would become their new home when they died. But isn't that just one more way of finding a permanent home in this world? Not a home of wood or brick, but an intellectual home. Not a home of obedience, but a home of insurance. A home not made of love for God, but a home of knowing that in the end I'll be OK. Not a home of hope, (because hope is trust in God), but a home of trust in the knowledge I have and the prayers I make.

When do we Arrive?

As we saw in chapter six, if we define pleasure as that moment at which we might say, "I wish this moment would last forever," then pleasure may involve a sinful effort toward making a home and seeking peace in this world. The quest for pleasure can become a quest for permanency, and permanency is impossible to attain. But the quest for permanency also has a spiritual, an other-worldly, element. It's the attitude that says, "Spiritually, I've arrived."

I have yet to find a place in the scriptures that teaches Christians to have this kind of attitude, or anything close to it. Certainly, there are passages where God speaks to someone and tells him that he's been chosen for something to do with His eternal will, as with the prophets or St. Paul. Perhaps someone like that has "arrived," although I think they themselves might disagree. Certainly St. Paul would! He wrote to the Corinthians "But I discipline my body and bring it into subjection, lest when I have preached to others, I myself should become disqualified."[52] He knew that even he, after bringing so many to knowledge of Christ, could still lose the very salvation he had proclaimed.

But does this even apply to you or me? Has God ever spoken to you from heaven and told you that He's using you to change history? I didn't think so. Me neither. So, since we're not in the class of Christians who hears the voice of God booming from the clouds, let's take a look at what the scriptures teach us and use that as our guide.

Our question is this: can I say, as a Christian, "I've arrived?" Can we say, spiritually, "I wish this moment would last forever," that is, "I've decided that if I die right now God has to accept me into heaven?"

Most people answer "yes" to this question. Of course, they don't say they're perfect, that they've "arrived" and have no sins with which to struggle, but many do indeed

---

[52] I Corinthians 9:27

believe that their salvation is complete and that they have nothing to add to it. They're in. Enjoy life until you die, then enjoy heaven. This is called "assurance of salvation," and it's a heresy. It says that if you become a Christian (i.e., you gain salvation); there is nothing you can do to lose that salvation. Sometimes it's called "eternal security."

Historically, the church has not taught this. The church teaches that salvation comes by way of the mercy of God, and no man can ever presume upon that mercy.

Is that even possible? How can a man presume upon the mercy of God? He would have to regard God as a machine – a machine into which one enters the right prayers and salvation always results. But I think such a person should be very careful in defining what he means when he calls himself a Christian. Saying Christian words does not make you a Christian. In St. Matthew's gospel, verse 7:21, Jesus tells His followers, "Not everyone who says to Me, 'Lord, Lord', shall enter the kingdom of heaven; but he who does the will of My Father in heaven." He who "does." Not he who did at one time. Not he who said. The Christian life consists of doing the will of God, and Christians are defined as those who do the will of God. Not those who have prayed certain prayers, attended certain sacraments, or belong to certain churches.

Read that verse again, St. Matthew 7:21: "Not everyone who says to Me, 'Lord, Lord', shall enter the kingdom of heaven; but he who does the will of My Father in heaven." How would one call Jesus "Lord" and not enter the Kingdom of Heaven? I mean, why or how would someone do that? This describes a person who believes that he is a Christian without being one at all, a person for whom the church comprises an intellectual, a family, an ethnic tradition, for whom the church contains no spiritual substance at all. Or perhaps a person who has abandoned the church and has become his own bishop, his own church. These kinds of people may refer to Jesus as "Lord", and never repent, never pray, never worship God in the least.

Hell will be very confusing for someone like this. He's believed all his life that he wants to go to a certain place, but if he went there, he would find that it's not at all what he wanted. He would find that people in heaven do not think like he does, no one there speaks his language, and he has no skills for the tasks he's asked to perform. Heaven is not where this man wants to be, but I'm guessing he's not going to enjoy hell that much either.

Now, I don't think of myself as a person who only pays lip-service to God, but I never want to take anything for granted. "The lamp of the body is the eye. If therefore your eye is good, your whole body will be full of light. But if your eye is bad, you whole body will be full of darkness. If therefore the light that is in you is darkness, how great is that darkness!"[53] Do you hear what this says? "If the light that is in you is darkness..." I may not understand this phrase completely, but I know one thing – it does not sound good. I know that there are many times when my eyes go places they should not, and so I might not call them good. But how can I tell? What if the inner light that I look to as my assurance of salvation is actually darkness, and I can't tell the difference?

See the unknowable quality of salvation, at least from a human perspective? It's not something you own; it's not a fixed commodity. It's not static. It's like anything that takes a great deal of practice. One day you think you've mastered it, and the next, you feel like you've slid back to "square one."

So with my Christian walk. Many times, I could accurately say, "I'm getting it," but then I fall into some stupid sin just a short time later. This is where I disagree with certain friends of mine who believe that they're already "saved" because of their confession of faith. If God is the only element in salvation, then certainly, I can believe salvation is always perfect. But He's not the only element in salvation. There has to be something to save, and that's me, and that means another element gets added. A very imperfect element indeed!

Salvation is a constant struggle. I don't rely on my own prayers and faith to get me into heaven, but on the mercy

---

[53] Matthew 6:23

of God and nothing else. And I'm not going to presume on His mercy either! Each day I seek it, ask for it, give thanks for it, rejoice in it, talk about it - but never presume upon it.

Repentance

Each day I repent for the many ways in which I do not deserve the mercy of God. Repentance, not assurance, is the key to heaven.

Repentance is a constantly churning sea whose waves throw us back to God, a stormy passage by which we hope to see mercy through the rain and fog. We can never say we've repented once for all time, or that we're saving up for one big repentance at the end. I hurt my back once leaning over a hospital bed for a full half hour listening to a woman give her final confession. She wept, she moaned, and most of the time I couldn't understand what she was saying. Except one thing was very clear: She was sorry she had waited all that time to reconcile with God. Is that the way to do it? Do you really want to assume that you will have a similar opportunity at the end? Heavens, no! Better to confess along the way, and make sure your priest's most lasting memory of you is something different than a sermon illustration about crippling back pain.

Every day, every week, spiritual rituals and practices must be accompanied by genuine repentance, or they're useless. David the patriarch told God, "For you do not desire sacrifice, or else I would give it. You do not delight in burnt offering. The sacrifices of God are a broken spirit, a broken and a contrite heart. These, O God, You will not despise."[54] Many times, I've gone to confession and found myself having to generate sorrow. I have to remind myself that I should feel sorrow for my sins. It's very easy to allow the rituals and prayers of the church to become routine, even those that themselves call us to repentance. It's very easy to lose sight of the whole reason for the church in the first place, and overlook the critical need for genuine repentance. It's also

---

[54] Psalm 51:16

quite easy to minimize the serious nature of sin because we do it so much. Recently, I tried paying close attention to something I do all the time – speeding. Have you ever tried following speed limits strictly? It started when I was riding with a co-worker, and I noticed that he somehow drove differently than everyone else. Then it came to me – he was driving exactly at or below the speed limit.

What a concept. I thought I might give it a try, and I noticed two things. First of all, I could see that I nearly always drive at least a little over the speed limit. As I attempted to pay attention to the speed limits and actually drive according to what they said, I sometimes felt like I was standing still. Second, I found that driving the speed limit really annoyed some of the other drivers. They didn't seemed to know what to make of someone driving the speed limit, and some of them tried stupid and dangerous things to try get around me, occasionally honking or gesturing as if I was the one doing something wrong.

It's the same with sin. When you decide to take repentance seriously, you find that there are dozens of things that you were doing that keep you separated from God, but you hadn't really noticed them in the past. In addition, you find that the world around you keeps right on sinning, and it may even come to hate you for the attention you give to avoiding sin and embracing repentance.

For instance, you might ask yourself, "What am I trying to accomplish when I talk?" and suddenly find that most of what you say is pointless and sinful. So you might try to be thinkful and reduce the amount of meaningless talking you do. But then others notice – "hey, you seem quiet today! What's wrong?" and so on. Sin, even when it doesn't know it's sinful, thrives and feeds on company. Sin loves company more than misery does!

The spiritual life does not have an ending point in this world. We begin on earth a process that will last for eternity – growth in godliness. Isaiah the prophet tells us, "For thus says the High and Lofty One Who inhabits eternity, whose name is Holy: 'I dwell in the high and holy place, with him who has a contrite and humble spirit, to revive the spirit of the humble and to revive the heart of the contrite ones."[55] Do you see what this tells us? God dwells in heaven with His humble and contrite followers, and His presence revives their spirits. Heaven is not a static place – in fact, I'll even go so far as to wonder if there will be confession in heaven, since there is no contrition, and no revival, without repentance.

We tend to think of heaven as a static existence because of the various kinds of entertainments that portray it in that manner. But your time on earth is like a time of gathering tools: repentance, knowledge of scripture, love for God, self-sacrifice. Heaven is the time when you come to use those tools to build your dwelling for eternity. Or, God's already built it[56], and you get to finish it off and make it your own.

It makes as much sense to say, "Well, I've assembled all the tools and materials I need to build my house. I guess my job is done," as it is to say, "I've said the right words to get into heaven. Now God has no choice but to let me in."

A Process

What do all these add up to? They tell us that we're on a path. Plato had it right in this sense – all of us are in the process of becoming. Only God is pure being, and some men decide to grow toward Him. No one has arrived yet. We reckon ourselves most accurately when we reckon ourselves as poor and hopeless pilgrims who are far away from where we're headed.

This process lasts throughout eternity. There is no end to it. You begin the process of journeying toward godliness in this world, and then continue it in the next. If you decide in this world that you do not want to participate, you have that option. But if you decide that God is the desire of

---

[55] Isaiah 57:15
[56] John 14:2-3

your heart, then you begin dwelling in the heavenly kingdom immediately. Eternity begins today and never ends.

Death, then, for the Christian, simply continues a process that each has already chosen for himself. The judgment, which is real, does not consist of a courtroom and a judge mulling over a huge file of all the things you've done in your life. Rather, the judgment consists of a continuation of your life on earth. If on earth you separated yourself from God, then you continue in that state in the afterlife. God does not reverse the decisions you've made day after day on earth simply because your heart stops beating. And if on earth you longed to know God as the highest of all pleasures, then you continue that same pursuit after your body dies. Think of everyone in the world standing on the top of a building. Death happens when you fall off. While we're on the building, some of us move toward the right side and some to the left. The side you're standing on when you fall off determines the place where you hit the street. You can't fall off the left side and expect to land on the right side of the building.

Everything, before and after, consists of a single motion in one direction.

A Contradiction

Here's the problem. Everything I've said, taken together so far, seems like a contradiction. After all, can a Christian live his life as if preparing for eternity in heaven, but at the same time constantly remind himself that he cannot presume to know if he'll actually get there? As an example of mental gymnastics, this seems almost impossible. Can I really prepare for my whole life to achieve something while at the same time continually reminding myself that I shouldn't expect to be successful?

This very paradox is the reason I say that we must reckon eternity to begin immediately. That we must assume there to be a very thin line between this world and the next. The reason most people believe that they want to go to heaven when they die is because they don't understand what heaven consists of. They think in very simply terms of heaven as paradise and hell as getting thrown into a bonfire. Which would you choose? Everyone chooses paradise, or at least almost everyone.

But heaven is not paradise as defined by this world. What would most men define as paradise? An unlimitedly secure future, that's what. Money and health – these are the things most people think about as paradise. Never having to worry. In a word: static. A check comes every month without my having to work at all. An unstructured life, free of worry or necessity. But heaven is not like that. The only way that heaven can be static is if we become perfect the moment we die. Certain religions, and even certain Christian sects have believed this through the years – it's called manichaeanism. They believe that the body is all bad and the soul is all good. That means we achieve a kind of perfection when the good soul is finally able to shed itself of the bad body.

But no, we don't become perfect when we die. Not at all. We continue to travel the journey of growing in godliness all through eternity. We continue to struggle and to grow in heaven.

Imagine you're standing in a church as the choir sings beautifully, the priest celebrates reverently, and you're caught up in the worship so that you can't imagine even heaven itself could possible satisfy your soul to any greater degree. Don't wish the moment would last forever, rather, pray for strength that you could take the closeness to God that you're experiencing with you when you leave the church and carry it throughout your life. This would comprise the pleasure of God, to know that eternity had manifest itself that moment in your heart.

Don't assume anything about the moment of your death, the judgment, or tomorrow. Don't assume anything about any point in the future. Rather, count yourself as having entered the Kingdom of Heaven at any given moment, and then decide to live the rest of your life there. This comprises our greatest pleasure. This comprises the pleasure of God for us. This is how we live in heaven continually without presuming upon the mercies of God.

8

WE LEARN TO LOVE PLEASURE BEFORE WE KNOW WE ARE LEARNING TO LOVE PLEASURE

*   *   *

What a joy to introduce children to the good things this world has to offer! Food, learning, entertainment, games and sports, sleepovers with friends, spending time with family members close and distant. We can all remember at least a few times when we discovered something new and the thrill we had of enjoying it. Children get to do that every day! A number of great memories come to my mind when I think about childhood. Kids in my neighborhood used to play street hockey on the street all winter long. I can remember playing one day when school had been canceled – not because of snow, but because it was very cold and they decided not to heat the school. We played all day, until long after dark when the only way we could see was by the streetlight reflecting off the snow. The cold made my feet numb, but I kept playing as long as I could stand. When I got home, man did they hurt! I cried all night long. When I woke the next day the radio said that school had been canceled again. I cheered as if my team had won the Stanley Cup, then ran outside to do it all over again. When school finally opened back up, some of the boys in the neighborhood had to stay home – sick and frostbitten!

But we were more than happy to pay the price. Not one kid would have done anything differently given another chance.

What pleasurable memories. And with them, I have less specific memories as well – coming home night after night, and dinner was ready. My mother washed my clothes, my dad paid the bills. I didn't know it at the time, but most certainly when you're growing up you live like a king.

We all want our children to be happy and healthy. We encourage them to discover and pursue things that make them happy, and we take them places that keep them healthy. Is there a problem with that? Well, everyone reading this may not have children, but everyone was a child at one time. Guess what? The fact that you love pleasure, sometimes to the injury of your relationship with God, was taught to you by your parents. Your parents! Oh, and if you're a parent, the fact that you love your children and want nothing less than the best for them sets them up for a life of struggle between the spirit and the flesh. How's that for bad news?

Of course, I'm not saying your parents are or were bad. I'm not saying you should, as a parent, deny your children the good things of life. We must give babies whatever they want, and take care of them, and provide for them.

There is a story of a king who was traveling. He came to an inn, and went inside. Instantly, the owner started putting out the best food and preparing the best room. But the king stopped him, and said, "I will not stay here if there is someone else staying here who has more authority than I do."

The owner exclaimed, "Your majesty! How can there possibly be anyone in the kingdom, much less in my humble inn, who has more authority than you?"

The king replied, "Babies. Babies have more authority than I."

How true. They come out when they want, they eat when they want, they sleep when they want, and if during their baptism they have anything they need to do, watch out! Hope you didn't wear your nicest suit!

Our early childhood fixes the love of pleasure into our minds before we even know there is such a thing as pleasure. For a baby, pleasures and needs are the same thing, and that's as it should be. When you were hungry, you screamed, and food arrived. When you were tired, you slept, and you let others worry about carrying you home. If you wanted one of your toys, you could reach for it and big hands would bring it to you. In short, for your first months, you would tell the world what you wanted, and the world handed it over. Not only were pleasures and needs the same thing, but someone met them (nearly) all the time.

This sets you up to believe something spiritually destructive: when you find something pleasurable, you feel like you can also say that you need it. And at some level, you also expect to get it. If you don't get it, you begin to feel like something is wrong with the world. Not getting what you want, which the infant inside you says are the things you need, makes you feel like you have lost control over the world. Like you're trapped in a high chair and can't get out, can't figure out how to get to the things that you deem important and necessary.

I include this as a part of the definition of pleasure that says, "I wish this moment would last forever," because much of our destructive pleasure-seeking comes from a longing to return to the carefree days of infancy and child-hood. As if those times, when you had no worries and got everything you wanted, could become permanent.

"Not me," you say, "I know enough not to think like a baby any more." Perhaps you do, but that makes you different than most people. Much of the thinking people do (especially when they're not being thinkful) has its foundations in the very basic moments and experiences of life. It's the thinking that says, "I can't afford this thing that I want, but I have a credit card so I'll buy it and worry about not being able to afford it later." Does anyone do this? Do you? "I like this person, and even though I should remain faithful to the person I'm dating/engaged/married to, I'll flirt a little because it makes me feel good." I wonder if this ever happens. Has it happened to you? Or, "What I want is more important than what the rules say so I'll just go ahead and do what's good for me." Has anyone you know ever said this? Have you?

It's supposed to happen that as you mature, you change the way you think. Parents hopefully begin the process of leading their children toward maturity even when they're still babies. Giving boundaries. Defining no-nos, and then as the children get older, giving more boundaries. They have to learn appropriate social interactions, about safety, how to brush their teeth. A difference between a quiet voice and a play voice, and when mom says no it means no.

Then the children get older, and we need to speak to them about "adult" pleasures, and how they may not enjoy them until they can make informed decisions. If ever.

But often, this process breaks down some-where. Why? Why do so many people remain immature? It's because the process of maturity is nothing more than a process of denying ourselves pleasure. Your first few months of life consisted entirely of pleasure, then life became progressively more complicated from there. After a few decades of this, when you have a job and a family, watch out! Many days contain nothing but work from dawn to night!

Most children understand the system fairly early in life. In fact, if a parent continues to give a child everything he wants for too long, the child will turn against him. Children have an innate knowledge that maturity involves self-denial, and they all, eventually, want to become mature.

As children realize this, they begin to realize the serious nature of sin. I've listened to many children's con-fessions in the past, and I can confidently say that even the youngest child understands the concept of maturity, of self-denial. Moreover, most understand that they've done wrong and need to be forgiven by God.

In fact, I can say that most of the children whose confessions I've heard have understood the gospel better than most of the adults. As our Lord has said, "suffer the children to come to me for to such belongs the kingdom of heaven."[57] Why did He say that? It's because our Lord understood that children want to enjoy things that are wholesome and good – they enjoy good pleasures. Have you ever seen a child get exposed to bad kinds of plea-sure? Cursing, pornography, fighting, drunkenness, and so on – children know that these things are wrong. They have a sense that these things are bad. My family went to a video store – once – that had an "x-rated" section separated from the main part of the store only by a curtain. As my wife and I looked for something our family could watch that night, one of the kids walked into that room. He instantly turned around and walked out with a face that looked like he had swallowed a cockroach.

But how long does that last? As children grow, they are exposed to sinful pleasures: smoking, drinking, drugs, sex, and criminal behavior. They know that these things are wrong, but they also have been trained to seek pleasure. It's like the wisdom they have as children gets buried under a wave of nostalgia for the past, when they got everything they wanted. Their parents taught them to pursue pleasure, and they continue to do that even when the things they find pleasurable have become the things they also know are wrong, are sinful.

But guess what? We have no choice but for this to happen. It's the nature of human beings to be sinful and to desire sinful things. Children must come to the realization at some point that they don't just do sinful things, but that they are sinful. They don't just do bad things, they are bad by nature. We as parents, again coming to the rescue, seek to keep that feeling from them as long as possible. I know that my wife and I don't want our children to feel bad about themselves, even though we regularly take them to confession. We wanted them to avoid bad things, but still feel good about themselves.

Of course, as they got older and we began to notice that large parts of their lives had gone completely outside our

---

[57] Mt. 19:14

control, we started to urge them to face the fact of their sinful natures.

They resist. All people resist hearing that news. It's as if we've told them for years that they're the smartest kids in the world and then have to break the news to them that they're riding the short bus. "Honey, I've always told you that you're the most graceful dancer of all, but from now on you have to wear this helmet to ballet class."

I once told a man that his eight year old son should come to confession. The parents had allowed their son to take communion at the Roman Catholic school where the boy was a student, and they were angry at me because I told them he couldn't take communion in our church as well. I told them that all the boy needed to do was come to confession, and I'd pray for absolution and give him communion that very same day. "It's an opportunity for your son and I to talk a little, which is a good thing. Believe me, he'll enjoy the experience."

"Confession?" the man yelled at me, "Confession? What possibly can an eight year old child have to confess?"

"Children are aware of their sins long before they turn eight years old" I said, "and besides, he'll learn that it's important to take communion in only one church."

But the child never came to confession or communion. When I saw him out in public some time later, his attitude toward me made it clear that his parents had told him I was a bad and dangerous man. For what, was communion the problem? Not at all. Every good Christian knows that he must choose one church and take communion there. Actually, the boy's father might have agreed with me if it had been anyone besides his son. So what was the problem? This dad didn't want to face the fact that his child had sins that would matter in a confession. He didn't want to think that he was already losing the control that he thought he had over his son. He didn't want the child to tell someone else family secrets. He wanted to keep his son from feeling that shame for sinfulness that accompanies every good confession.

Selfishness and Thanksgiving

Ok, we've got the blame placed securely, and surprise! It landed on mom and dad. Of course, fixing blame doesn't help very much, it only allows us to make excuses for our behavior. "As a child I felt like all my desires should be fulfilled, and they were. Therefore, I'm addicted to giving in to my desires." Much psychological counseling is full of blame placing, and it leads to nothing at all that resembles healing.

But it's true. All of us at some level to return to a happy and carefree childhood, even if we didn't have one ourselves. And why? Because we didn't need much to be happy and all that we needed was granted quickly. I call these "infant pleasures" – food, people, sleep, warmth. We do no wrong in wanting those things, certainly, but infant pleasure-seeking has an additional characteristic that fills us with sin. Infants assume that the world revolves around them. The baby assumes this because of a lack of awareness – he has no idea that others around him may have desires of their own that they want fulfilled as much as he wants his. So, the infant pleasures have no moral characteristic of their own, but the way the infant seeks and expects them introduces a moral issue – selfishness.

The first lesson we receive from our parents is: be selfish. Again, no one has a choice in the matter. The baby cannot be anything but selfish and the parents cannot do anything but respond as totally submissive slaves to the selfishness the baby exhibits. But as we introduce our children to more and more of the world, we expect that they will shed some of their selfishness. That they will become more aware of others. They won't give up the good memories of infant pleasures, the needs we all have that enable us to live, but we want them to begin to care about other people.

This brings us to adult pleasures. Now, by "adult" I don't mean "for mature audiences only." "Adult pleasures" refers to anything beyond the infant pleasures: meaning, renewal, community, and so on. We do no wrong in wanting those things either. Our sin lies in the degree of selfishness we carry over from our infant years. If you reach out and grasp for meaning (or renewal, or community, or any of the other adult pleasures) the same way a baby reaches for the loudest and most brightly colored rattle, you haven't matured at all. Sure, you can read and drive a car and follow the stock market, but you're really just a baby. You believe deep inside that the world revolves around you, you've just come to understand that you can't push too far or the world won't revolve around you the way it should anymore.

Selfishness has levels. A baby is totally selfish and maturity is a process of becoming less selfish, but we cannot say that someone has achieved perfect maturity only when he's achieved total unselfishness. Total unselfishness is useless, and a totally unselfish person would not be able to live.

When my son first started playing soccer, he passed the ball every time it came to him. He thought everyone else was better than him, and that he would be a good team player by passing the ball to the players who could score goals. So when I took him to games I started asking him, "Who is the best person on your team to dribble the ball down field and make a goal?" He would grudgingly answer, "me," meaning himself, only because he knew I wouldn't let him get out of the car until he said that. And guess what? His talent at the game improved greatly, the team scored more goals, and everyone had more fun.

Balance Selfishness

How could I say I helped my son in his journey toward maturity? Didn't I, the parent, simply add to my child's im-maturity by encouraging his selfishness, at least as regards the possession of the ball in a game of soccer?

Yes, but only if I also kept him from the balance upon our selfishness, thanksgiving.

St. Nicodemus of the Holy Mountain was influenced by, and used the writings of, an Italian spiritual writer, Lorenzo Scupoli. In the book *Unseen Warfare*, originally written by Scupoli but added to by both St. Nicodemus and Theophan the Recluse, the second chapter has the title, "One should never believe in oneself or trust oneself in anything." I must confess that I often find myself approaching the writings of the church fathers with great fear and trepidation, and chapters titles like this are the reason. How can I go through life not trusting in myself? Would a man even enter a monastery or study for priesthood unless he had the confidence to know that he could rise to the challenge?

Of course, you have to read *Unseen Warfare* to really understand what St. Nicodemus was saying. This line explains it best:

> For know and understand, that in this unseen way all are losers except a man who never ceases to struggle and keep his trust in God; for God never abandons those who fight in His armies, although at times he lets them suffer wounds. So fight, everyone, and do not give ground; for the whole thing is in this unceasing struggle.[58]

"So fight," he says. This sounds like he and I would agree more than that chapter title suggests. I want to strive, to better myself, to achieve great things, to accomplish goals, to gather resources for good use, to give my talents in the great struggle against evil – all while looking to God as the source of my strength.

> Looking at yourself or at other people and thinking that you alone have been given high rank, that you alone of all living beings on earth have the gift of reason, and serve as the point of

---

[58] Scupoli, 89

union and connection between material and immaterial creatures, rouse yourself to glorify and thank your God and Creator, and say: 'O eternal Trinity, Father, Son, and Holy Spirit! Be Thou blessed for ever! How greatly must I give Thee thanks at all times, not only because Thou hast created me out of earth and hast made me King over all earthly creatures, nor only because Thou hast honored my nature with Thy likeness, with reason, speech and a living body, but above all because Thou hast given me the power, of my own free will, through virtues to resemble Thee, that thereby I may posses Thee in me and rejoice in Thee for ever![59]

Only a mature man could pray this prayer. It contains within it a healthy self identity, one might say even a certain level of selfishness and bravado, balanced by the firm belief that all strength, intelligence, expression, perseverance comes from God. And how is that belief expressed? In thanksgiving. This prayer comes from the lips of one who has become his own parent. The fact that he enjoys, even pursues, the infant pleasures does not force him to embrace infantile selfishness. He can thus pursue the adult pleasures always with reference to giving thanks to God.

So my soccer playing child learns to keep the ball a little longer and thereby gets better at the game. He learns to score goals that give glory to his team, enjoy the fellowship his effort generates, and gains confidence in other areas of his life, all while thanking God for the talent and health he has been given.

Here's my point: Don't kick yourself for the fact that earthly pleasures constantly tempt you. Don't kick yourself for realizing that – when you don't think – you automatically grab at pleasures like a baby in a high chair. Don't blame anybody or any thing.

---

[59] Scupoli, 131

Give thanks. Persevere. Expect that the end of the struggle can never arrive, certainly not in this world.

Fr. David R. Smith

9

THE LORD'S PRAYER
AND PLEASURE

*   *   *

What have we learned about pleasure so far? We've learned that desire fuels pleasure, that pleasure can get out of hand when we're not thinking, that sometimes it consists of nothing more than our attempt to avoid pain. We've learned that pleasure becomes self-defeating and sinful when linked to a longing for permanence. These are all the rather complicated aspects of pleasure, the kinds of things that we can't overcome easily or quickly.

But pleasure is also something very simple. A glass of water, a sunset, a favorite easy chair, talking with a friend. These things have no great moral characteristics of their own, but they bring to our lives wonderful moments of joy.

I visited a monk one time to confess my sins. When we finished, I told him I needed to leave immediately and drive a long way back to my home. I was in a rush. He told me that he didn't want me to drive on an empty stomach, took out an apple, and began cutting it up. We ate it together. We didn't talk. I could see that he was, at that moment, the happiest man in the world: serving, eating, being quiet. That apple tasted very good.

But another person could have cut an apple apart that same afternoon in a house in the same village as the monastery, and the cutting would not have brought any joy at all. The person may have hurried, may have hurt himself with the knife, may have been arguing with someone else in the house. You see? It's not the action that makes the pleasure, but the attitude that accompanies the action.

We want to cultivate this attitude. If we can train ourselves to take pleasure in the little things, then denying ourselves pleasure in other, destructive things might not present so much of a challenge. During Lent, for instance, I might find myself sitting in front of a salad when I really wish I could eat pizza. So what can I do? I can thank God for the salad, and rejoice in it before I begin to eat. Thank God for each bite. But then later that afternoon I find I'm hungry long before I normally begin to think about dinner. Now what? Look for the little pleasures. I might think back to the salad, ahead to dinner, about the things around me that make me content and give my life meaning. It's not the same as prime rib, but it gives me what I need to keep the fast joyfully, to give thanks continually, to see God's grace and mercy in everything. Many times, I'll have an apple.

Now, don't allow this example to trivialize this aspect of the spiritual life. Seeing the grace of God in everything is a difficult virtue to cultivate, even though it focuses on the little things. Some people try to cultivate this virtue by trumpeting a false sense of wonder at everything, to the point that they become annoying. A man I knew would say "Oh, thank you Jesus!" and "That's so special!" and things similar under his breath constantly. I don't want to make fun of him because he was a very pious Christian and a good friend. But the whole thing seemed rather trivial and contrived. Even if he held no pretense in saying these kinds of things, it still seem labored and false.

On the other hand, I knew a family whose young son had been killed in a car accident. I prayed a memorial at the grave with the parents some years after the funeral, and as we walked back toward our cars the mother said, "It's all been a great grace, father. It's all been grace." I could never get tired of hearing that. She had most certainly learned to find pleasure in the little things of life, because big things had been taken away.

Finding pleasure in the little things is a very serious matter, a virtue for serious seekers-after-God to cultivate. But how? How can we train ourselves to look around at the good things God has given us with a constant sense of wonder and thanksgiving? Well, I suggest we take a prayer that we pray often, several times each day, and make it a prayer of pleasure. The "Our Father," the Lord's Prayer. Let's see if we can use parts of that prayer to bring our minds into line with the virtue of taking pleasure in the little things of life.

Our

"Our Father," we say. The first word of this prayer always stuck me as somewhat out of place, "our." I pray this prayer several times each day, but very rarely do I pray it in the presence of other people. So who is the "our"? Is this prayer only for the monastics, who pray it most often in church, where the "our" describes all those gathered? Perhaps Jesus gave the prayer to His disciples with the intention that they would only pray it only in a group?

No. I think there's a different reason altogether. We may pray in private, but we are saved in the community of the church. The good members and the bad, the old and the new, the attentive and the slothful – our Lord looks on us as a community of believers. Certainly, each one of us must approach the Lord as individuals. We don't come to the judgment as a group. But you cannot decipher the Christian life on your own. You need the wise to teach you and the fools to trouble you. Without both, if you're missing one or the other, you crash like a plane with only one wing.

Of course, the wise are the easy ones to get along with. It's the fools that are part of the "our" that give us trouble. A priest once said to me, and as we rode in my car, "I just wish I had a church with no problems." Just as he said this we passed an empty and dilapidated church building. "There's a church with no problems," I said, and we both had a good laugh.

"Our Father." We can pray these words while alone, but we do not pray them by ourselves. Even the hermit living in the hollow of a tree, who speaks with no one but the angels and animals, even he prays these words as part of a community of believers. He occupies a place in that community, we need him and he needs us.

This point is significant as we consider the relationship of Christianity to pleasure. My fourth definition, and the eleventh chapter of this book, addresses the supreme importance of communion with other persons as the highest expression of pleasure. This means communion with God as well as with other people. But it suffices at this point to say that the first word (or second in some languages) of the most-prayed prayer of the Christian faith must bring to mind those multitudes of people who have influenced our spiritual journey. This does not come easy, and the task weighs heavy on the single small word that carries it. Especially when we're talking about the negative experiences.

When most people have anything to do with someone who genuinely challenges their sense of themselves as good, their first reaction is to try and cut off contact with that person forever. Break up the relationship, quit the job, move out of the apartment or neighborhood, shun the family member. In my job, I have many opportunities to warn people about their work performance. I like to do this, because it gives an employee a chance to correct his behavior and not only keep his job but also contribute to a more productive and joyous workplace. But most of the time, people don't like to get warnings. They defend themselves, they yell, they cry, and more often than not, they tell me that they're not going to work for me anymore. Why? Wouldn't a person want to work for someone who cared enough to help them and instruct them in how they could do their jobs better? No! Most people see themselves as nearly perfect under their particular circumstances, and the person who says, "No, that's not the case. You have room for improvement," is the person they feel they need to get away from as quickly as possible.

The same phenomenon happens in families. I also have many opportunities to interact with families, and often encounter shattered relationships. The problem is that you can't choose your relatives, especially your brothers and sisters, and many folks find themselves thrown together by the necessity of having to make financial and healthcare decisions when mom or dad needs nursing home care. What has happened in the past that these family members hate and distrust each other so much? Most of the time, these feuding siblings seem to be very similar in character, although they would be very angry if anyone said so. Because they're so similar, they see their own faults in the other. Who wants to visit and talk to someone whose very appearance reminds you of your faults – the same ones that your employer warned you about and your spouse complains about? The ones who want to avoid facing their faults at all costs become siblings who "aren't talking."

The process of ridding ourselves of those people who try our patience happens in a continuum, from minor behaviors like merely avoiding the person to the most extreme level, that is, murdering someone so that they will never again remind us of our flaws. But it's all the same continuum. You've been on it. I've been on it. But whenever we pray the first words of the prayer, "Our Father," those people come back to us. When they do, we have to look at ourselves as the problem. Not some of the problem. Not half the problem. The problem. And no one has the time, since the insight lasts the length of only one word, to think about how we would have done things any differently. No. The word "our" says this to us: all the people in your life to this point have made you what you are today. The ones you haven't met yet will continue to mold you. When you forget that the process is meant by God to be one of the greatest pleasures of life, even when it's nearly impossibly difficult, you continue to miss the gift, the mercy, and the grace He has in store for you.

Daily Bread

"Give us this day our daily bread." When we looked at the matter of permanence, we discovered that much of our pleasure-seeking comes from a desire to have everything "set" for us forever. A bank account fat enough to never have to worry again. The kids out of the house and pension checks arriving every month. No problems.

When we say the words "daily bread," we counteract that longing for permanence within us. When we say "give us our daily bread," we give God permission to give us only our daily bread. No more. That's why the word "daily" is in there. My "daily bread" means that I can live for the day God has given as His gift and mercy to me, but also means that I will have to come back to Him tomorrow to ask again. And the next day as well.

Imagine that someone said to you, "I will send you five hundred dollars every day for the rest of your life. The only catch is that you have to call me up every day and ask for the money. If you miss one day, the deal's off." How would you regard the daily phone call you needed to make to ask for the money? I'll tell you. You would structure your life around that call. Around making sure you're near a working phone. Making sure you're awake and aware, that you never, ever, forget to make that call.

Now, imagine that you've made the call every day for five years. Almost two thousand calls. You've received almost one million dollars from this deal, but what starts to happen? You want more, of course! You become lazy and greedy. Perhaps you say you need more than five hundred dollars a day. Perhaps you tell the person giving you the money that you'd rather make one phone call each week and get $3500. Perhaps you decide it's not worth it because you don't like being beholden so much to another person. Perhaps you get bored.

Why? Because even when we're "set" for life, we want more. Even when someone asks us to do very little to gain a great deal, part of us bristles at being told what to do. The thing that makes you feel like a king at the beginning soon makes you feel like a performing dog.

This same emesis of pride rises in us when we pray the Lord's Prayer thoughtfully, and rages against the words "daily bread." Something inside us says, "I really don't only want my daily bread. I'd rather have bread for the long run, and then I could relax a little and enjoy life." And, although our inner voice avoids adding this, it's still there: "...and I wouldn't have to rely on God." Given the choice between God's mercy and a fat bank account, many would choose the money.

But not you! As long as you pray the words "Give us this day our daily bread" thoughtfully.

Trespasses

Trespasses. I like this word better than "debts" because we can enter debt legally, but trespassing is never legal. "Trespass" means that you've gone somewhere you shouldn't have gone.

Isn't this the essential element of the discussion of Christianity and pleasure? That we all simply do things that we shouldn't do, go places we shouldn't go, and say things we shouldn't say? And we know it! The law of God has been written in our hearts, no matter how much we smother the voice, and this law speaks to us words of warning when we cross the line into territory that has been posted with the sign, "No Trespassing."

When it comes to a discussion of those pleasures that hurt our relationship with God, the word "trespasses" urges us to view them spatially. An alcoholic knows he should not go into a liquor store, a bar, or the home of someone who urges him to drink. If he's in a bar, he's not temped, he's dead.

The temptation happened outside the bar. When he walks in, he's already trespassing. I knew someone who was an alcoholic and would often go to bars. He said he wouldn't drink, and that he went there to talk and play pool and whatever. Of course, his whole life consisted of a parade of stupid decisions, and continuing to go to bars was just another one of the same. Trespasses. There are places you shouldn't go.

I know another man who decided to stop using a computer in his home. He had to use one at work, but at home he would often find himself spending large amounts of time reading meaningless garbage, viewing web sites that he shouldn't have been, buying pointless "collectibles," and playing games. When he decided he didn't want to do those things anymore, he determined to limit the amount of time he spent on the computer. But it didn't work. Soon, he went back to his old ways. He needed to think spatially when it came to sin. He needed to make the computer itself a "trespass."

This influences the way we gain pleasure from the little things of life because we have to decide where we can go and where not to go. Did you ever have a place you knew you just shouldn't go? When I was in college, I had an acquaintance who was a wild man. His parents had a large family business, and so he thought that college would be just one long vacation. Whenever we would get together, things got crazy. He only lasted one semester, thanks to God. After my friends and I got to know him, we all tried to avoid seeing him, especially toward the end of the week. His idea of a fun weekend was a "road trip" to the wrong end of town, and we soon learned that we didn't want to try and keep up with him. His room was off limits. We tried to stay away – at the risk, literally, of our lives.

This is the meaning of the word "trespasses" in the Lord's Prayer. As you go through your day, and try to avoid the places where you know you should not be. Trespasses. Thoughts you shouldn't have. Temptations. Halls you shouldn't walk down and people you shouldn't talk to. Task number one is to identify them, and task number two is to avoid them. Then give thanks to God! Take pleasure in the little things – the light God has shed in your soul, the wisdom to avoid sin, the strength to steer clear of the pitfalls, and the forgiveness that allows you to start again when you fail in the effort.

The Evil One

Pleasure belongs to everyone. It is the will of God that we experience pleasure while we dwell on earth, and He has given us wonderful gifts that fill us to overflowing with thanks for His goodness and grace toward us. The evil one cannot stop that, so he attacks God's people by making them believe pleasure is a bad thing. He loves miserable Christians. Unhappy, suspicious, advice-spouting Christians. They are the junior members of his sales division.

The process starts when the evil one fills us with a longing for those things that we know are contrary to God's will – trespasses. We know that our parents would not want us to give into temptation, that the church wouldn't want us to, that they are as wrong as wrong can be, and yet we still feel like we want them. What creates that desire? Is it simply human nature? Not at all. The Evil One has servants who suggest to you that you want certain things, and fill you with distractions so that you forget other things. Satan can't keep you from experiencing pleasure, since pleasure is God's gift to us, but he can ruin it for us. Like a bully bending the wheel of your new bike so that it rolls with a jitter, Satan takes the good that God has given and tries to get you to twist it into a shape he enjoys.

"Deliver us from the evil one," we pray. We do not ask God to destroy Satan, but only to keep us away from him. Deliver us. Make him stop telling us that the things that will kill us are actually good for us. We know he lies all the time, and we pray for the strength to stop listening.

But then the process continues after we avoid the pitfalls the devil has placed in our path if we then deem all pleasures to be trespasses. This happened at the time of the scriptures, as St. Paul tells St. Timothy, "Now the Spirit expressly says that in latter times some will depart from the faith, giving heed to deceiving spirits and doctrines of demons, speaking lies in hypocrisy, having their own conscience seared with a hot iron."[60] Read that again. What would you think would come next? That these people who had departed from the faith who gave heed to demons would – what? Engage in terrible and immoral acts? Perhaps perversions beyond what a normal person could imagine? Sounds appropriate – but no. This is what they do when their consciences are seared with a hot iron: "...forbidding to marry, and commanding to abstain from foods which God created to be received with thanksgiving by those who believe and know the truth."[61]

These folks didn't find new and exotic methods of debauchery; they established new heights of self-denial. And what does St. Paul say of them? They have departed from the faith. St. Paul's does not desire the followers of Jesus Christ to embrace a life of misery and privation, but to recognize in everything around them the blessings, the mercy, and the pleasure of God.

St. Peter learned this lesson as he prayed upon the roof of a house in Joppa. He saw a vision, something like a sheet descending, and upon in all kinds of animals. A voice told him to eat of the animals there, and he piously replied that he would not – he would eat nothing unclean. The voice said to him, "What God has cleansed you must not call common."[62] Now, this passage's deep meaning has to do with the inclusion of the Gentiles in the Kingdom of God. But there is also a more practical and immediate meaning as well: St. Peter could eat pork and lobster. This may not be the most significant event in salvation history, but when I thank the Lord for breakfast and enjoy a slice of bacon, in connects me

---

[60] I Timothy 4:1-2
[61] I Timothy 4:3
[62] Acts 10:15

to the story from scripture that teaches that the gospel is for every person, every culture.

When we pray, "deliver us from the evil one," we indeed pray, "do not allow Satan to take from me either of two things – my discernment that some pleasure is bad for me and my certainty that not all pleasure is bad for me."

Fr. David R. Smith

10

POPULAR ENTERTAINMENT

*　　*　　*

Some years ago I ran a retreat for a large group of young people. During a question and answer period, one of the girls asked me if I thought Christians should listen to popular music. I asked her to quote me the first line of her favorite song on the radio. She became rather embarrassed, but after some encouragement she recited a line. As soon as she said it, everyone started talking – about the song, about the artist who recorded it, and probably about how shocked they were to hear that line spoken aloud in a church. The words were clearly suggestive. When I repeated the line, the energy in the room rose another couple of levels. I asked them what the line meant. No one would answer. I repeated it. Was it about eating breakfast? About buying a car? I kept saying it over and over again, asking them to tell me what it referred to. Every time I quoted the line, the noise in the room increased. The nervous whispering became talking, then nearly shouting. Finally, the bolder ones answered me – the line referred to sex. No one could interpret it as referring to anything else.

Truthfully, I knew it referred to sex, and the fact that much of the popular music that young people listen to refers to sex doesn't surprise me at all. The excitement of courtship and marriage certainly have a place in the cultural expression of any people. But the line she quoted referred to more than sex. It was, I found out later, from a rap song that had nothing but obscene and perverse lyrics – and for what purpose? Other than as a quick way to make money for the artist and producer?

A couple of things struck me about this exchange, which I hadn't planned at all. First, almost everyone knew the rest of the words to the song the very moment the girl said the first line. Of course, the same could have been said of my own generation. If a priest had said, "take a sad song," to the young people in my church when I was growing up, every single kid would have responded, "and make it better." Second, the fact that the song referred to sex seemed to surprise everyone. They hadn't thought about it before. Of course, everyone knew at some level what the song was about. But again I think back to my own youth. The song, "Let's Spend the Night Together," clearly referred to sex. We all knew that. But on another level it was just a song that didn't apply to us and had no moral value. Perhaps things are the same today. The kids at the retreat knew what the words of the song meant, and that those words didn't belong in the church. But they didn't feel like it was out of place in the church because it referred to sex. No. They felt that it was out of place because the words meant nothing to them and didn't fit into the atmosphere of life-forming lecture and discussion that comprised the retreat that weekend. The words of the song carried no weight in their lives but the words in the church carry all the weight that words can possibly carry.

At least that's what I hope they were thinking. You more cynical readers may roll your eyes at my naiveté. Yes, some of the young people there that day listened to, and probably still listen to that music for the fact that the words fly in the face of everything their parents and the church teach. But most, I think, had simply listened to that song without thinking at all – until that day.

My interaction with this teenaged retreatant contains four characters that comprise a full discussion of Christianity and pleasure as it relates to popular entertainment. First, the people assembled, **the crowd**, represent the culture in which we live, which produces the popular entertainment we consume. Second, **the girl** represents the individual forming her likes and dislikes in a sea of choices. Then **the song** is the message that popular entertainment preaches. And last, **the priest** is the church sparring with the culture in which it lives. Sometimes the sparring is friendly and graceful, almost like a dance. And sometimes it's not friendly at all.

The Crowd

Popular entertainment is an expression of the world view of a culture, and reflects, to some degree, that culture's self identity. In the same way that the total of a man's life comprises the man, not only the good words he speaks but the base thoughts he has, even the most unwashed elements of cultural expression still express something of the character of all the people of that culture. You may look at certain programs on TV or hear particular kinds of music and say that they do not to express your own sense of your self at all; however, they still exist as a part of your – our – culture, and therefore some part of them reflects some part of you.

In order for Christians to free themselves of the culture in which they live, they must form another culture. A counter-culture. They need to live outside the culture without moving to another geographical location. Some Christian denominations do this, even considering their counter-culture identity as their central characteristic. In the part of New York where I live, there are many Amish farms. They interact with the broader culture only as much as necessary for their survival, and no more. They dress differently than everyone else and ride around the countryside in buggies drawn by horses. Their children don't go to public schools. This is an easy example of a counter-culture.

"Certain passages of the New Testament seem to support this kind of attitude. Our Lord Jesus Christ told us that the way is narrow that leads to life, and few there are that follow it."[63] If the few are the members of your group (and the "many" of verse 13 describes everyone outside your group) this passage certainly makes sense. But what if God doesn't draw the line exactly where you do? If not, well then the counter-culture idea really doesn't work. When we form a counter-culture, we must affirm that some people – in fact, most people – will never access the gift of salvation. If Christians were to establish their own unique culture, we would have to admit that the Christian message does not apply to everyone. We would have to admit that those who do not embrace the externals of a Christian culture – clothing, food, music – place themselves outside of God's plan for salvation.

Does that make sense? No. The gospel must be made available to everyone, not contrary to the prevailing culture but a fulfillment of it, a healing of all cultures and all people. We must try as much as possible to make the gospel apply to everyone in the world, regardless of culture. The love of God, not clothing, music, or food, must determine who comprises the "few" and the "many."

But we must take care in this matter. We may certain deem some kinds of clothing and music characteristically Christian, and some parts of every culture are clearly non-Christian. How can we decide?

St. Paul offered the Corinthian church some advice in this matter, and his words pertain to us as well. "I wrote to you in my epistle not to keep company with sexually immoral people."[64] This is clear. If the culture in which you live regards sexual immorality as an acceptable form of entertainment (which ours does), then he seems to be saying that we must separate ourselves from it.

---

[63] Matthew 7:14
[64] I Cor 5:9

That's simple enough, but St. Paul adds something more: "Yet I certainly did not mean with the sexually immoral people of this world, or with the covetous, or extortioners, or idolaters, since then you would need to go out of the world."[65] Did you hear what he said, "go out of the world?" This complicates matters somewhat. He told the Corinthians that they should avoid the sexually immoral person, but that they should not and cannot establish their own "world," their own culture. This sounds like the old "be in the world but not of it," one often hears. But does that really capture the fullness of what the scripture says? I don't think so, in part because of what comes after: "But now I have written to you not to keep company with anyone named a brother, who is sexually immoral, or covetous, or an idolater, or a reviler, or a drunkard, or an extortioner – not even to eat with such a person. For what have I do to with judging those also who are outside? Do you not judge those who are inside?"[66]

The key is this: we judge people. Not culture. And we don't even judge all the people. We judge ourselves in the church, but do not judge those outside the church. St. Paul says nothing about the culture per se, other than that we cannot establish a culture outside the world in which we live. But we don't judge cultures. Those who are Christian are judged by a strict rule of conduct, and those who are not Christian are not judged at all (at least by us. As he says in the next verse, "But those who are outside, God judges").

We don't judge cultures, even our own. We judge people, starting with ourselves, by asking this question: What kind of a person has our culture created? How have I been influenced by my culture? If you can live in the culture but not have its evil influences harm you, like a nurse caring for a diseased patient taking careful precautions not to contract the disease herself, you do well. But when the microbes get under your skin, you have a problem. Then you have to rely on those in the church to judge you so you can repent and return.

---

[65] I Cor. 5:10
[66] I Cor 5:11-12

Why does this so rarely happen in the actual practice of the church? The answer is easy. Many churches, especially in North America, have come to regard being non-judgmental as the highest good. Everyone welcome, no strings attached. Why? It's because churches compete for people, even churches of the same denomination. Every pastor and church leader has to have the most friendly and open attitude possible, not only no only in order to spread the gospel, but also in order to maintain a viable church. He has to try and strike the balance between enforcing the obvious standards of the Christian faith and finding people to join and stay in his church. Which of these two often gets overlooked? Sad to say, pastors often lower the standards of the faith, or are directed to by higher authorities, in an effort to keep people coming and giving.

Sometimes, a priest find himself trapped between the parishioners and the higher authorities, both urging him to relax and get along. I myself have had this happen, when I told a man that he could not come to Holy Communion because of some piece of unfinished business in his life. He called the bishop, and the bishop called me. I didn't get yelled at, but I didn't get supported, either. The man was doubly angry because when he appeared the following Sunday in the communion line, I told him I still wouldn't give him communion. I don't say this to scandalize you, but listen: don't become a source of sadness and despondency to your priest. One of the jobs of the church is to judge you. Let the church do its work.

Back to the question of culture. Ask yourself how much the culture of the place where you live affects you. Do the attitudes of the culture draw you away from your relationship with God? If you can genuinely say "no," and you have no fear to discuss the question with your spiritual father, then what, I ask, is the problem with listening to the music you like or owning a TV?

The Girl

The girl represents the individual forming her likes and dislikes in a sea of choices. In our society, choices are market driven. If enough evil people want a particular thing to be available in our culture, they will get it. The same holds true for the good.

Therefore, we contribute to our culture by consuming those things that we regard as good, and avoiding those that we deem evil. Every time you step outside this pattern, I mean to say, every time Christians support the evil by their consumption, they add to the degradation of the culture.

Can it be said that the girl who asked me that question at the youth retreat was a consumer of evil? Well, there are several answers to this question. First, yes. She admitted listening to music that clearly espouses a lifestyle contrary to the will of God. Second, no. She listened to the music on the radio, but because of her critical listening to and concern about the lyrics, would not purchase the music or attend concerts by the artist. Third, yes. She knew the words, and had flooded her mind with their attitude by memorizing every line of the song. And fourth, no. Her life and faith did not reflect the attitudes of the song. She liked the beat and the tune, but the artist had not won her over to his way of thinking. She regarded the sub-culture of that genre of music as shallow. In the struggle between the evil of the music and God's goodness, God had won.

I have to believe that she felt guilty for listening to that music, or she wouldn't have asked the question. But I also thanked God as soon as I understood her struggle. Guilt is good when it makes you take a hard look at your life. I personally don't think she was guilty of anything, but if feelings of guilt forced her to consider the evil attitudes of the words in that song, then – bring on the guilt!

Why do I say this? Not because I want this girl to suffer needlessly. Rather, I believe that something happens when you begin to listen carefully to the words of songs, or to think about the attitudes expressed by the entertainment you enjoy. Understanding that the music you enjoy has an evil message destroys the attraction, at least it does if you care what message you listen to. I grew up listening to music that's now called "Classic Rock," and I sometimes enjoy listening to that kind of music on the radio. But now I listen more carefully to the words than I did as a younger man, and when I hear something that disagrees with my present attitude about things, I find that the song has lost its appeal, and I turn the radio off. It happens often.

The Song

The song is the message that popular entertainment preaches.
I very much enjoy looking at popular entertainment theologically. I would love if more people did. I saw a movie called "Slingblade" (1996) some years ago. As I remember, a mentally disabled man had committed murder when he was a boy, and the movie begins with him as an adult being released from the institution where he had grown up. He ends up living with a single mother and her son. This woman has a boyfriend who is no good – selfish, childish, and he treats the boy badly. One day the disabled man and the boy go fishing, and they have a very powerful theological discussion. They essentially decide that there are certain sins that can not be forgiven. Murder is one of them.

When they return to the house, the disabled guy decides that the best way he can pay back the woman for her kindness toward him is to kill the no-good boyfriend. Since he couldn't be forgiven for one murder, what was wrong with committing another? His standing with God would not change at all. So, very calmly, he kills the boyfriend with a lawnmower blade as the two of them sit in the kitchen. Afterward, he calls the police and sits down across from the boyfriend's body to eat a biscuit with mustard on it.

Wow. Popular entertainment with bad theology! I told a friend about the movie, and when I was done he told me that he had seen "Slingblade" and hadn't picked up on the theology in it. I told him I wished he saw theology in every movie he saw!

Another time, I saw an episode of the TV program "Everybody Loves Raymond." Ray's wife tells him that his oldest daughter has some questions about life, and Ray gets a stack of books that teach parents how to talk to their children about sex. He goes to her room and asks her if she has a question. She asks him "why are we born?" Ray starts to answer the question "how are we born," but she stops him. She already knows the answer to that one. What she really wonders is why people need to be born if everyone goes to heaven anyway[67]

What a great question. What a lousy place to ask it. Ray goes downstairs and his wife, brother, and parents engage in a very humorous exchange, trying to figure out the answer to the daughter's question. One starts to read the Bible from the beginning. Someone tries to get the priest on the phone. Robert (his brother) becomes spooked by all the deep philosophical pondering.

But what about the girl's question? Of course, I shouldn't have expected a good answer to emerge in the context of a half hour sitcom. When Ray decides to go up to his daughter's room again, he finds her playing with her siblings, apparently having forgotten all about why people are born. He and his wife stand in the doorway, smiling at their children, with looks on their faces that say, "enjoying children is the meaning of life." Yikes. What's the real message? "If the children begin to talk about God, distract them and they'll forget about it." The next day, a woman where I work gushed on and on about the episode, trying to convince me that anything that mentions God, or any prime-time program where some words from the Bible are read, must be good. I didn't know how to even start responding to her.

Recall, if you saw it, "The Hunchback of Notre Dame", the Disney version. Those people in the church, what were they doing? Praying the most selfish prayers imagin-

---

[67] Everybody Loves Raymond, "Talk to your Daughter" Season 6, Episode 19

able. My children complained every time they watched that movie because I stopped the tape (the old days of VCRs) at that point to have a discussion about how wrong it was. Does everyone who prays only pray selfishly? "No, Dad. Now can you turn it back on?" And Pocahontas with the new-age teaching, talking to wise old trees and so on? My heavens! I had to get rid of that one, because I would have had to stop the tape every few minutes.

Does this mean that popular culture espouses an evil gospel? Not at all. Recently I saw an odd movie called "Nacho Libre" in which the main character prevails against overwhelming odds by praying. It's the same with the old version (stay away from the new one) of the film "The War of the Worlds." I enjoy watching "The Santa Clause" every Christmas just to hear the lines, "Sometimes believing in something means you just believe it," and, "Seeing is not believing, believing is seeing." I know many will laugh at me for saying it, but I think these are two of the finest lines in American cinema.

I'm sure you can think of some examples where you've seen theology, good and bad, expressed in popular entertainment.

Popular culture does not preach any consistent message. It's up to those of us who consume popular culture to determine for ourselves what message the song, film, program, book, or magazine proclaims. It's up to us to help our children, or children in general, take the time to think about the entertainment they're consuming. When you watch TV or a movie, you let the producer fill your head with images. Sometimes it's funny and meaningless and harmless. But other times the producer, writer, or actors have an agenda that they want you to join. Their souls are rotting, and they can feel it, and they think they can feel better by getting you to let your soul rot as well. What do you think? Do you want to let them?

The Priest

The priest is the church sparring with the culture in which it lives. Sometimes the sparring is friendly and graceful, almost like a dance.

For thinking Christians, the message conveyed by popular entertainment determines the extent to which we enjoy the experience. The same holds true for the Corinthians, as St. Paul seems to indicate in another part of his first epistle to them. They obviously participated in the culture of their city, and their spiritual father never told them to stop: "All things are lawful for me, but all things are not helpful."[68]

You see? The standard that St. Paul brings to the question of Christianity and pleasure asks this: Is it helpful?

When we allow ourselves to be entertained, we allow someone else to control where our mind goes. We must, therefore, engage in all forms of entertainment critically. One must make oneself aware every moment of the work's message, of where the artist wants to take your mind.

Sometimes the artist wants to take your mind to places your mind should not go. That's when the sparring between the church and the culture becomes less of a dance and more of a street brawl. Remember the movie "The Last Temptation of Christ"? Christians all over the country protested outside movie theaters. At that time, a man who owned a movie theater that showed "The Last Temptation of Christ" came to our church. I was serving as a deacon. The priest threw him out of the church and told him never to come back unless he was willing to repent of making money on that film. When the man refused to leave, the priest threatened him with violence.

I was very impressed. How many priests would have the courage and conviction to do something like that? This must be the true standard by which the church relates to popular culture – in a word, engage critically. When the

---

[68] I Corinthians 6:12

cultural expression is harmless, no problem. When it becomes spiritually destructive, problem. Then the church must have the courage to stand up and make the will of God known.

*   *   *

In our discussion of Christianity and culture, I urge Christians to learn to enjoy the little things. Those of us alive today have the technological option of enjoying popular entertainment twenty-four hours per day, easily. Is this a great opportunity to enjoy the little pleasures of life? We must always be willing to ask ourselves if what we're consuming is helpful. We must ask: Is what I'm consuming right now drawing me closer to God, or pulling me away?

11

THE HIGHEST PLEASURE

*   *   *

You've stuck with me so far. Thank you. I know this has been a bit like a long flat climb up a steep mountain. I hope a couple of good views have opened up along the way. But now at the top, we come to the end of the matter – the greatest pleasure of all, the supreme joy of being a human being. Nothing more lies above the point where we stand right now. Nothing is ever better than the view from the peak.

My fourth definition of pleasure, "pleasure is communion with another person," contains every other definition of pleasure, but it also contradicts all of them. How can it be that a woman who literally weeps from fatigue still rises from sleep to comfort a crying child? How does a man run headlong into certain danger in order to save another – even someone he may have never met? The decision people make to give of themselves brings them joy, even though suffering and sometimes death may accompany it. And in some cases, *because* suffering and death are included. The moment of giving rises from, and gives rise to, gratitude and peace, the experience of communion, a prelude to all life that follows, the birth of a relationship, the noble act which becomes a standard of character. Sometimes the sacrifice gives birth to a relationship with the person who has benefited, but sometimes not. Either way, a communion develops between the giver and mankind, or between the giver and God Himself. Nothing enriches relationships like sacrifice.

In what way does this contribute to our discussion of Christianity and pleasure? How does the sacrificial, communal experience of pleasure relate to the other, simpler forms of pleasure? In order to answer this, we must constantly ask ourselves a question: How we can focus the pleasures we love toward the relationships that most nourish our spiritual lives?

We can get started with the gospel story of the Rich Man and Lazarus.[69] In this story, a rich man who lives in a beautiful home, wears beautiful clothing, and eats good food every day, dies. At the same time, a beggar named Lazarus who would lie at the rich man's gate and fight with the dogs for scraps of food also dies. The bulk of the story consists of a conversation between the rich man and the Patriarch Abraham concerning the character of the afterlife:

> And being in torments in Hades, he lifted up his eyes and saw Abraham afar off, and Lazarus in his bosom.
>
> "Then he cried and said, 'Father Abraham, have mercy on me, and send Lazarus that he may dip the tip of his finger in water and cool my tongue; for I am tormented in this flame.' But Abraham said, 'Son, remember that in your lifetime you received your good things, and likewise Lazarus evil things; but now he is comforted and you are tormented. And besides all this, between us and you there is a great gulf fixed, so that those who want to pass from here

---

[69] Luke 19:19-31

to you cannot, nor can those from there pass to us.'

"Then he said, 'I beg you therefore, father, that you would send him to my father's house, for I have five brothers, that he may testify to them, lest they also come to this place of torment.' Abraham said to him, 'They have Moses and the prophets; let them hear them.' And he said 'No, father Abraham; but if one goes to them from the dead, they will repent.' But he said to him, 'If they do not hear Moses and the prophets, neither will they be persuaded through one rise from the dead.'"[70]

Abraham's first answer to the rich man's request for water can easily be interpreted as saying that those who experience pleasure on earth pay for it by going to hell, and that those who are denied pleasure on earth are reimbursed by an eternity in heaven: "Son, remember that in your lifetime you received your good things, and likewise Lazarus evil things; but now he is comforted and you are tormented."[71] The afterlife, from this perspective, simply consists of the opposite of one's experience on earth, at least as it relates to pleasure. Every moment you suffer on earth drives your soul ever upward and every good experience stokes the flames of hell a little hotter.

This interpretation might give those who suffer some hope about the future. But what of those who do not gain hope from Abraham's words? I mean, those who identify more with feasting sumptuously than with dogs licking their sores? Clearly, the story makes us (because if you're reading this now, I'm assuming you have more in common with the rich man than with Lazarus) feel a little guilty about the pleasures of life we enjoy, right? Abraham seems to say to the

---

[70] Luke 19:23-31
[71] Luke 19:25

rich man that the fact that he lived a life of pleasure in this world caused his condemnation. Is he also deliberately allowing Lazarus to overhear his words, hoping that he will learn that the suffering he endured on earth caused his salvation?

I don't think so. After all, imagine if things had gone a little differently. What if the rich man looked out his window and saw Lazarus, went out, chased away the dogs, cleaned his sores, and brought him inside for a plate of that sumptuous food. What would happen then? Should Lazarus have refused to come, seeking to suffer as much as possible in order to gain heaven? And yet, it seems like that's what Abraham would have wanted – for the rich man to help Lazarus. But would that have caused Lazarus to suffer all the more in the next world? Perhaps the rich man's charity would have endangered Lazarus' place in Abraham's bosom. How, in that case, would help help at all? Worse yet, perhaps Lazarus would stay at the rich man's house and eat the good food, dressed in some nice clothing while the rich man went out to find other men who needed his charity. Then if they both died at that moment, their places in the afterlife would come up exactly the opposite from the gospel story. Lazarus in hell, perhaps a tummy ache rather than fire torturing him, and the rich man in Abraham's bosom. Hardly the goal of charity, to be sure.

This doesn't make any sense. The enjoyment of pleasure was not the problem the rich man had. The story teaches us that his selfishness, his neglect of the poor man outside his doorway brought about his condemnation. If this were not the case, why would Jesus tell us about two men who lived in the same place and died at the same time? The story could have illustrated that pleasure in this world equals suffering in the next by saying: "There was a rich man who died, and of course, since he was rich, he went straight to hell." But no. This rich man had a poor man suffering on his very doorstep, and he did nothing about it.

There has to be something more in this story. Abraham tells the rich man that he's suffering because of all the pleasure he experienced on earth. But why does he not address the subject of charity? One answer might be that Abraham had heard the rich man say, while alive, "Look at that man out in front of my house. What a lazy bum. He deserves to suffer, and I (who work hard for my money) deserve to have pleasure." For the rich man, this was a statement of justice. One can hear an echo of this in the rich man's words from the story – he tells Abraham to give Lazarus things to do. It's like he's finding Lazarus a job. "I recognize that bum in your arms, Abraham. He hung around my place when I was on earth. Hey, I'll tell you what, I have something for him to do. Tell him to get me some water, that'll get him out of your hair for awhile. What's that? He can't? Well, then send him back to earth to talk to my brothers. At least then he'll be good for something." The rich man sees Lazarus only through eyes of justice, or commerce. Abraham's answer turns his own attitude of justice back upon him: "You had pleasure while he suffered, now he gets pleasure and you suffer. It's only fair."

But there is something much deeper in our Lord's teaching beyond the fact that the rich man withheld charity from Lazarus. One must be struck by the de-personalization of the two main figures – the rich man in his house eating and Lazarus, close by, outside suffering. Perhaps both of them thinking about the issue of pleasure with no reference to the other man. Even after the two of them die, they do not speak to each other at all. This deepens the lesson behind the story of the rich man and Lazarus – our Lord is telling us that we must speak to one another. We must spend time with one another. The rich man's sin was not primarily the pleasure that he experienced or the charity he neglected to show. It was the reluctance he had to invest any of his life in Lazarus' life.

We learn this lesson only through great effort. I decided before Thanksgiving one year that our family would go to a program at a local church and help them serve a big traditional meal to the poor and disadvantaged. I expected that it would give my children some sense of their own blessings, since they would see first hand the poverty of some of our neighbors. Of course, I knew that this never really works. Children become thankful for what they have only when they get old enough to understand what goes into making money and buying things. Sure enough, while we served the meals I could see an insurmountable wall between the people who came to the dinner and my children. They waited on the tables, and smiled, and said "Happy Thanksgiving," but they said nothing more at all and had no concern for the people other than filling their cups of coffee and asking which kind of pie they wanted.

I'm not even talking about "communion with another person." I would have been happy with one extra word. How difficult it can be!

What starts in youth often continues throughout one's life. I've said before how I often need to deliver written warnings to underachieving employees where I work. The job really belongs to other members of my staff, but I've found that they do everything in their power to avoid it. Why? Because showing people how to do their job better is not nice? Because the charges on the written warning are not true? No, not at all. People hate this job because delivering a written warning to an employee forces you to engage that person. Emotion will pass between you. Perhaps you'll look deeply into one another's eyes. Uncomfortable silences happen. Perhaps some yelling. Only very rarely is it clean and quick and pleasant. Normally, communing with another person in this context takes a great deal of energy.

Energy is really what we're talking about. Why don't we spend time speaking with people heart-to-heart? It's not a lack of time, it's a lack of willingness to spend energy. We simply don't want to take the effort to be charitable, other than to send a check now and then. Is that enough? The story of the rich man and Lazarus calls us not only to practice charity, but to embrace a life of charity.

Perhaps some of you are thinking that the parable of the rich man and Lazarus has nothing to do with relationship building, only with God's desire that we show charity to those in need. If you're thinking this, let me tell you why I disagree. I believe that communing with people, taking the time to know people, putting energy into people, showing love above and beyond simply practicing charity puts us closer to the will of God. I can show you a thousand people who have charitable hearts whose afterlife will be identical to the rich man's. And why? Because charity does not equal a love for God, or even a love for mankind. People practice charity for a multitude of reasons, many of which have nothing to do with their spiritual lives. And while I can show you a thousand whose charity cannot save them, I ask you to show me one man who could – being in the same situation as the rich man in the gospel – step outside his house to speak heart-to-heart with Lazarus and not decide to help him in some meaningful way. Could anyone do that? No. Now certainly, a conversation with a poor man (or any other charity) cannot save anyone's soul from eternal death and separation from God, not at all. But I'm saying that genuine charity happens in some kind of relationship, some kind of sacrifice, some kind of giving up the energy you don't think you have. Some kind of experience of the pleasure of communing with another person.

The Final Pleasure

Ultimately, the relationship that we must built most carefully, the relationship in which we must take the most pleasure, is our relationship with God. To take a good look at this, let's look at the scriptural story that I think most illustrates the relationship of Christianity to pleasure. This is the essential Biblical passage for our whole discussion, the story of the foolish landowner in St. Luke 12:16-21.

> Then He spoke a parable to them, saying: "The ground of a certain rich man yielded plentifully. And he thought within himself, saying 'What shall I do, since I have no room to store my crops?' So he said, 'I will do this: I will pull down my barns and build greater, and there I will store all my crops and my goods. And I will

> say to my soul, "Soul, you have many goods laid
> up for many years; take your ease; eat, drink,
> and be merry.'" But God said to him, 'Fool!
> This night your soul will be required of you;
> then whose will those things be which you have
> provided?'" So is he who lays up treasure for
> himself, and is not rich toward God.[72]

It is from this passage that we get the phrase, "Eat, drink and be merry." Well, let me qualify that. We get the Biblical instance of that phrase in this passage from St. Luke, but we don't get the idea. For the philosophy of pleasure as the highest good, we have to look to the Greek philosopher Epicurus. But don't think of Epicurus as a real-life version of the foolish landowner. Epicurus viewed the pursuit of pleasure as the highest good, but the pleasures he had in mind were not the pleasures the scripture warns us against.

Epicurus urged his followers to pursue what we might refer to as "higher" pleasures: "direct every preference and aversion toward securing health of body and tranquility of mind, seeing that this is the sum and end of a happy life."[73] In other words, Epicurus viewed pleasure in terms of pursuits that would result in a healthy body and a tranquil mind. Learning. Exercise. Belief in God. Fearlessness in the face of death. These were the higher pursuits for Epicurus, and living a life of pleasure meant living a life of striving toward these things.

Of course, the first thing people think of when they hear Epicurus' name is food. Today, the word "epicurean" describes a person who enjoys good food, and by extension, the "finer things of life." How did this happen? I don't know how, but I do know this – whatever took the name of Epicurus from the philosopher himself to the base reduction of his philosophy into "wine, women, and song" had already happened by the first century. The concept that life is nothing

---

more than the pursuit of one fleeting pleasure after the other had captured many at the time of Christ's ministry on earth, and the parable of the foolish landowner from St. Luke's gospel gives our Lord opportunity to expose the debasement of Epicurus' philosophy for what it was, and still is today.

I mean to say this: the pursuit of pleasure as the highest good (I'm speaking in hyperbole. The highest good is the pursuit of God) must not automatically be dismissed by the pious Christian. We simply need to consider the definition of pleasure, we need to identify the joys that pious Christians experience as pleasures, and thereby bring joy to our lives by recognizing that God has given us great blessings on this earth. To the "higher pleasures" of Epicurus we may be so bold as to add other categories, like suffering persecution, loving the unlovable, physical ascesis. And others, like the smell of a church when you first walk in the door. Teaching children about God. Sacrifices that result in immediate and knowable good. The joy of the great feasts.

Above all, knowing that God knows you. And loves you, and showers you with mercy when you ask. That he's prepared a place for you – you're living there now, and later on, He has another one that's even better.

What Makes the Foolish, Foolish

The foolish landowner does us a great service by illustrating, one at a time, each of the four definitions of pleasure. By getting them all wrong, his pursuit of pleasure provides us with an example of what not to do.

Look at him. He shows us how we sometimes pursue pleasure by focusing upon desires that we believe might be satisfied in the future – pleasure as desire fulfilled – by making his plans about his barns. "I will pull down my barns and build new ones," he says. In other words, the foolish landowner finds that he dares, because his crops have yielded such an abundance, to long for everlasting prosperity. He reasoned that the barns would carry the wealth he experienced from one successful harvest into future years, and even beyond that.

On how many different levels does this not make sense? The storage of crops is certainly the most tenuous of capitol investments. But our Lord knew that. This parable uses the least permanent form of wealth to illustrate the temporary nature of all wealth. No matter what you have, no matter how secure your future earnings, one bug, one fire, one bad year can wipe it all out.

When we rely upon, or are forced to rely upon, something that provides everlasting prosperity, we endanger our souls. One experience comes to mind. Every city has certain churches, huge downtown Protestant churches, the places where rich people worshipped fifty or one hundred years ago. Today, some of them still open their doors every Sunday, but in some cases only because they survive off of large endowments.

I spoke at one of these churches some years ago in order to raise money for a project I was involved with. I went into the sanctuary on the Sunday morning I was to speak – vaulted, gothic, magnificent old dark wood, but no people. I thought perhaps I had arrived at the wrong time, and sat down in a back pew to read a hymnal. After about a half hour, I started walking around the building, and soon found the "congregation," a small group of grey haired folks, in what looked like the old Sunday School auditorium. I apologized, gave my little speech, and they presented me with a check.

Afterwards I asked the pastor what was going on. He told me that they didn't like worshipping in the sanctuary anymore. Having so few of them sitting in the big open space was depressing. But how, I asked, did they still remain open? Endowments. The church could afford a staff of seven with a congregation of not many more than that. Their endowment stated that some of the money had to go to a local charity every year, and that's how the donation for my project came about. I've thought occasionally about that experience over the past twenty years. It was like entering a cave full of spider webs and lizards. The church is closed now.

Money, like the crops in the parable, is just one more commodity. It can enhance a spiritual life or destroy it. It can bring pleasure or it can bring about spiritual death. But how? In the case of the heavily endowed churches, relationships become fractured. If a church has to fight to stay alive, relationships are absolutely necessary. Everyone must work together. But when a church begins to collect money and investments, the need to cooperate and to love one another stops. The pleasure becomes worldly and stiff. Catered dinners and mink coats. No one can experience pleasure as communion with another person in such an atmosphere.

The landowner also illustrates the second definition; pleasure is that moment at which you say "I wish this moment would last forever." But what does he wish would last forever? Nothing other than his moment of prosperity, and our Lord tells us that he laid up treasure for himself as a way of forcing that to happen.

Of course, one does not break the law of God by establishing a savings account and adding to it regularly. But as with his plans to build new barns, the treasure-laying of the foolish man sapped all the life from his soul. He could feel the fatigue inside himself, and urged his soul to ignore the problem, "Soul, take your ease," he said. Who was he talking to? The scriptures say he spoke to his soul, but ordinarily we do not address our souls as entities distinct from ourselves. So who's he talking to? Himself! Our Lord describes the perfect dialogue for the man who refuses to pursue the pleasure of communion with another person – it is nothing more than him talking to himself.

Many people talk to themselves. I've been embarrassed many times driving my car, talking to myself, praying, practicing a sermon, when someone sees me from another car. I don't know why I worry about it at all – those who know me are probably not surprised that I talk to myself and those who don't know me can think whatever they like.

But the man in the parable does more than talk to himself, he counsels himself in spiritual matters. This is very different than simple self-conversation. I have decided many things while talking to myself that don't seem very smart when I describe them to other people. The foolish landowner was a self-counselor, and the counsel he received virtually ended his life.

How often do I, as a priest, receive the news that someone has made an important, life-changing decision without consulting any spiritual guide! And usually, it's too late for me to say anything, to make a difference. Normally the person has no concept of asking a spiritual father about big decisions, and expresses surprise that I would even suggest such a thing. Some even think I'm introducing a new idea into the Orthodox Church. They roll their eyes and say to one another in a language I can't understand, "He's a convert. He doesn't understand the way we do things."

They are the same as the foolish landowner, who counseled with himself by talking to his soul, and believed that the words he said were true and good, when they in fact destroyed the very soul to whom he purported to speak.

After he illustrates to us the first two definitions of pleasure, and how exactly a careful person would not pursue pleasure, he moves onto the third. The foolish landowner tells his soul that it should satisfy itself, "eat, drink, and be merry." In other words, make the little things of life, the passing pleasures that God has given to us in His supreme mercy, make them the very essence of life. Make the least important into the most important.

Some TV programs and in movies try to create humor out of those who replace important issues of life with the unimportant. Who care nothing for the future in order to satisfy some fleeting whim. Who hurt others in order to get some meaningless thrill. Who are knowingly and extremely arrogant without shame. Who are wealthy and enjoy acting condescendingly toward others.

Who just don't get it.

We laugh at these jokes because they remind us of people we know, and if we're honest, also remind us of ourselves. When the foolish landowner says, "eat, drink, and be merry," he's really talking about a permanent vacation, a life without worries. Who hasn't wished for that at one time or another? And yet, look at him. Just when he thinks he's firmly rooted in a life of Epicureanism and merriment, his soul is required of him and he cannot rise to the challenge.

Finally, what is really the biggest problem the foolish landowner has? His small barns? His belief that his good harvest will support him forever? His assessment of life as nothing more than food and fun? No. These are his problems, but none of them are his biggest problem. Our Lord gives us the answer to that question when he tells the multitude listening to Him, "So is he who lays up treasure for himself, and is not rich toward God."[74]

Rich toward God. Now that's a phrase from the scriptures that I could never grow tired of hearing. Rich toward God. It's not money that has destroyed his soul, it's his neglect of his relationship with God. There is nothing wrong with building barns, with saving money, with eating and drinking, with being merry. But there is something seriously wrong if you do not nourish your relationship with God every day, every moment of every day, through the pleasures you pursue and experience. The man who saves his money and feeds his relationship to God is wise. The man who saves money and neglects God makes for himself an eternity of suffering and death.

---

[74] Luke 12:21

Fr. David R. Smith

12

THE ESSENCE OF THE MATTER

* * *

As soon as my mother died, the nursing home where she lived called to tell me. It was jut before six in the morning, and even though I was driving to work, I was also still half-asleep. I didn't reply at all to the news. The nurse asked, "Are you all right?"

"Oh. Yes, I'm fine. It's just so early," I answered. To be honest with you, I was relieved. My father died in 2001 and my mother in 2006, and during the five years between those two dates my mother and I fought constantly about her living conditions and her quality of life. She had elected, as many older folks do, to stay in her home. But she stayed much longer than she should have, beyond the time when it became dangerous for her to be living alone. I couldn't stop her, because that's what she wanted – to sit in her own chair with her own TV, to eat whatever she wanted and go to bed when she decided she felt tired.

I argued with her constantly about going into a nursing home. When I would visit her, the house was filthy and smelled terrible. She tottered through the rooms unsteadily with her walker, and I could see that she had clearly eaten nothing but candy, wine, and popcorn — no actual meals. She never took her medications at the right times, and I found out at one point that she basically gave money to anyone who asked for it.

"You can't live alone anymore. It's dangerous and pointless. You'll be better off in a nursing home."

"No. I'm leaving this house feet first and no other way."

Well, she left feet first, but not in the way she expected. She fell three times in two days and the ambulance came and took her to the hospital. She didn't want to go, because I had told her that if she fell and got hurt I wouldn't let her live in the house anymore. At the hospital she kept telling me how she would "be more careful" when she got back home, ignoring everything I had said (and was still saying) to her about the fact that she would go directly from the hospital to a nursing home.

The first day in the nursing home was not good. She would not get out of bed, would not eat, would not watch TV. She wanted me to know that she hated it more than anything.

A few days later I had an activity at church and afterwards went to visit her. She looked like a whole different person. Her color was back, her face fuller and eyes brighter, and she had certainly regained her willingness to fight.

"I took the altar servers bowling tonight," I said to her.

She scoffed. "I went bowling too," she said, as if her bowling trip was better than mine.

"Wow! That's great!" I wanted to know how they got her out to a bowling alley.

"It was right here," she said. "It's a little lane with a little wooden ball and little pins and I got the best score." The way she spoke seemed to say, "Don't you know anything?"

I was amazed at how much she enjoyed it. "Wow, that's great. And you look great, too! I guess the nursing home has been good for you after all."

She looked at me and squinted her eyes, gunfighter-style. "No," she said, "It hasn't. I don't like it here at all."

It turned out that she was much sicker than anyone had imagined, and she only spent a couple of weeks in the nursing home before I got the call that early morning on the way to work. But I'll tell you, those were the best two weeks (of the last five years) of her life. She felt better, enjoyed the company of other people, went to church, ate three good meals a day, and so on – things we thought she would never do again. She wouldn't admit that she liked it, but she did. I genuinely thank God that she was in the nursing home when she got very sick – I'm sure she would have still fought with me about going anywhere besides her home.

This situation with my mother illustrates how pleasure can be summed up in one swift and ever-present act: choice.

I could see my first two definitions of pleasure every time I visited her when she was still living alone, where I would see her, virtually every time, sitting in her easy chair and watching TV. That state, that position, had become the sole occupation of her life, and she wanted to do nothing except maintain that position as much as possible in the years after my father died. She was never happier than when she was sitting in a chair and watching TV, and living alone simply meant that she had the opportunity to do it all day and often all night. If pleasure is desire fulfilled, my mother had relinquished all desire to the one act of sitting and watching. And if pleasure is that moment at which you say, "I wish this moment would last forever," my mother experienced that kind of pleasure every day, and nearly every hour of every day.

How critical it is that we choose what we desire! Had you asked my mother as a young woman, as a wife and mother, even as an old woman – at any point in her life – what she wanted more than anything, would she have answered, "I want to sit in a chair, watch TV, and do nothing else?" Not at all. Not a chance. When she was young, she wanted to get married, have a family, and maintain a happy home. That was a concrete desire, one that she could have expressed if asked. But what happened to her concept of what she desired when she achieved the things she had longed for? What do you want after you get what you want? The answer's easy. She had no idea. She just knew that, in earlier years, after a long day of cleaning, cooking, washing and providing, it felt good to take a little break and watch a game show or soap opera. Then what happened? The little break became all day, and no "work" got done because she had decided she'd done enough work in her life. She became addicted to the TV.

I wanted to make sure that my mother had a good quality of life in her final years, and to me that meant she would exercise, take her medicine, go to doctor's appointments, get out and visit people, and generally speaking, engage living. But that's not what she wanted. She wanted to be left alone. Oh, she got lonely sometimes if people didn't come to visit, but when I stopped to see her she would often complain that too many people had come to visit and that they had stayed too long. Her idea of a perfect social life was one short visit from one person each day. Then she could watch TV. She liked it when my children came to her house and did nothing but watch TV with her. I would try to get them to talk to Grandma, and she would tell me to leave them alone. Spongebob was as good as Bob Barker.

When we define pleasure as desire fulfilled, when we seek to control what we find pleasurable by seeking to control what we desire, we do well. But the moment we stop doing this, both desire and pleasure begin to deteriorate. Desire becomes unfocused, as in the Proverb, "The soul of a lazy man desires, and has nothing."[75] Our souls never stop desiring. The question then becomes not, "do you desire anything?" but, "who or what decides what you de-sire?" Who chooses what you desire, what gives you pleasure?

Eventually, I gave up on my mother having a good quality of life according to my standards. I thought for awhile

---

[75] Proverbs 13:4

that she may have been depressed, and took her to doctors to see if this was the case. They agreed that she was depressed according to their criteria. But she said she wasn't, or at least she refused to anything about it, and then wouldn't go to that doctor's anymore. She took some pills to solve the problem, but that was it.

"You're depressed because you live alone and don't eat anything," I would say.

"Yeah, well, then I'll be depressed."

So she sat in her chair and poked the button on the remote. She was content. She wished that moment would last forever. But did it? Obviously not. With no exercise and poor nutrition, and blunted social stimulation, she became sicker and sicker until the day she couldn't get out of her easy chair at all. After trying to get her to do something about her condition, I finally had to buy her a motorized easy chair that tipped forward when she wanted to stand up. But her health continued to deteriorate to the point where she couldn't stand at all, and when the chair tipped her forward it simply poured her out onto the floor.

I know that many people self-destruct through inactivity, but I never really knew what was involved until I found myself responsible for the person doing it. It was very unpleasant. She would sit and watch TV and wish the moment would last forever, and I would see her sitting there and know that everything was falling apart. No moment lasts forever. My mother is a perfect illustration of the futility of saying, or living as if you're saying, that any moment can last forever. She would get very frustrated at the things that kept her from doing the one thing she wanted to do, and I would warn her that her deteriorating health would soon make even the simple act of sitting in a chair and watch TV impossible.

You see, my first definition of pleasure, that pleasure is desire fulfilled, calls us to choose what we want. When you don't do that, you become a victim to whatever image blows your way on the wind of laziness or advertising. But then, when we decide what we want, we have to work for it. The second definition of pleasure, a moment we wish would last forever, calls us to work for what we want. Calls us to admit that there is no rest in this world. The nice things you desire begin to deteriorate the moment they becomes yours, and without constant attention and effort, will eventually make any and all pleasure impossible. The soul of a lazy man desires, and even if it gets what it wants briefly, it soon has nothing.

Then it was time for her to leave her home, and she knew that she would never return. The first two times she fell, she told the ambulance drivers to put her back in her chair and leave. The third time, her doctor came to the house with the ambulance and told her that she needed to give it up and go to the hospital with them. My mother concurred.

She wasn't stupid. She knew that as she got into the ambulance that day, she would never see her home again. Can you imagine that? She had gone out of the house very few times in the five years previous to her hospitalization. Her world was defined by the four walls of her living room, by the sound and jiggly light of the TV. Then on that day everything changed. The front walkway, the stretcher, the ambulance, the hospital. Waiting in cold and impersonal rooms. And after some days, the nursing home. A small bed, a roommate, chattering nurse's aids telling her what to do.

If the issue of Christianity and pleasure comes down to one thing – choice – then how could my mother find pleasure at all in these events? Her choice had been taken away from her, first by poor health and then by, well, me. But had choice been completely taken away from her? Is choice ever really taken away from anyone at any time? When I went to speak with her at the nursing home, I urged her to try and find joy in her surroundings. Activities, church, meals, and so on. Ultimately, I think she did, although she wanted to appear as if she had no choices or opportunities so that I would feel as badly as possible about putting her there.

I work in a nursing home. Sometimes I think about our residents – about what it would be like to work my whole life to have a home, a profession, a family, accomplishments, and then to end up with half a room and the necessity of living by someone else's schedule. Will I be able to choose to take pleasure in the parts of my life where pleasure was still possible? I hope so. I try to give our residents as much choice as possible, hoping that the process of choosing itself will result in a more joyous and pleasurable life. But I know for many of them, finding joy and pleasure is a monumental effort. I think it was for my mother. I think it would be for me, and for you, too.

Someone said to me that my mother was playing the part of a martyr during her stay at the nursing home. The person who said this meant to commiserate with me, to make me feel better. But the more I thought about this statement, the more I hoped it was indeed the case. The martyrs had so much taken from them, so much pleasure denied. But that was their choice! Certainly, it's easier to decide to look for pleasure in the little things when the end of your life arrives during a stay at a nursing home than it would if the end came by a flame, the tearing claws of a lion, or the point of a sword. But the same process of choice is required.

The Heavenly Mother

Now from the earthly to the heavenly.

I look at the example of my earthly mother and try to determine how I might have done things better, and how I might even now do things better. Who can give me some direction, some help and guidance? My spiritual mother, Mary, the earthly mother of our Lord Jesus Christ.

One would not ordinarily think of the life of the Theotokos and Ever-Virgin Mary as an example of a life of pleasure. Spiritual fulfillment, yes. But pleasure? Didn't even Simeon the Righteous tell her that a sword would pierce her soul, foretelling the crucifixion of her only son?[76] How much pleasure is there in the life of a single mother today, and wasn't it worse in first century Palestine? And yet we can see her wise choices concerning pleasure along every step of the

---

[76] Luke 2:35

way, when she agreed to bear God Incarnate, and as she raised him from infancy to manhood.

When the angel came to Mary and told her the plans of God for her and her child, after going over some points for clarity, she said to him, "Behold the maidservant of the Lord."[77] What wonderful words these are! How joyous and pleasurable our lives would be if we learned to say them every day!

If you asked the Theotokos what she desired the most, she would not say that she wanted marriage, a family, a nice house. She would have said that she wanted to serve God. She would have said, "behold the servant of the Lord." Her desires were formed according to His desires, like aluminum foil wrapped tight against a golden chalice of inestimable value.

I confess that I often do not give myself to God in this way. Too much, I find myself saying, "I believe that my desires are in accord with the will of God." In other words, I decide what I want and then check to see if God would give me the "OK." By this way of thinking, of course I should have gotten married – I wanted to, and listen to the wedding service, how it says that at the Wedding in Cana of Galilee God sanctioned marriage. Of course we should have had children, that's what married people do, and Jesus Himself said that children should be allowed to come to Him. Of course I should have a nice house and eat good dinners. Didn't Jesus enjoy a good dinner in Zacchaeus' nice house?

These plans start with me, not with God. I do not say, "behold the servant of the Lord," rather, I say, "here's what I want, God. Is that OK?"

The Theotokos perfected the relationship of Christianity to pleasure by making her every desire God and God alone. She took pleasure in the mercy, truth, and glory of God. "Do not be afraid, Mary," said the angel, "You have

---

[77] Luke 1:38

found favor with God."[78] God looked at Mary, and was pleased. Is he looking at you now with pleasure? At me?

The Theotokos must have been a peaceful and patient mother. She knew that sadness was coming her way, as Simeon had said, so she must have been in no hurry to see her son grow up and become a man. And yet, she did not try to stop Him, either. On the contrary, she hurried God the Father and God the Son at the Wedding at Cana, forcing our Lord to change water into wine.[79] Pleasure, to her, never meant that she would say, "I wish this moment would last forever." No, rather, the scriptures tell us that she "kept these sayings in her heart;"[80] that is, she put the moments of Christ's life together in her mind in order to work out her own salvation and that of the whole world.

The Theotokos did not try to stop time. I think the present day obsession with photography and video taping are a symptom of our desire to hold things still – especially in relation to our children's lives. We don't keep things in our hearts, we keep them in digital format. My children's school sells tapes of sporting events. Tapes of high school lacrosse and soccer games! Why would I want to purchase such a thing? Even when one of my children makes a goal, do I really need to hold onto that forever on tape? Should I buy it for Grandma and Grandpa, fully knowing that they would do nothing except fast forward to see the moment of the goal, and then put it away? Oh, I'm as proud as any other parent when my child does great things in school – let me tell you about some of them sometimes. But nothing lasts for-ever. The children continue to grow, and the same love, attention, support, direction that went into the game winning goal in eight grade must continue throughout the child's life.

I want to be like the Theotokos, and treasure these things in my heart. Not to wish I could stop time, but to take delight in the moment, continually seeking the will of the God for every moment that comes after. To seek salvation.

---

[78] Luke 1:30
[79] John 2:1-11
[80] Luke 2:51

Then, eventually, the moment came that had been foretold by Simeon, the moment when she stood watching her only child die on a cross. Would it have been possible for the Theotokos to "call off the deal" as she stood and watched her Son and our Lord suffering that day? By that, I mean, could she have said to God that she really didn't want to give her only Son for the salvation of the world, that she would rather live a normal life, to look forward to grandchildren? Who knows. But I've got to believe that had she had made such a decision, we would not honor her as much as we rightfully do. I have to believe that this decision, had she made it, would have resulted in some kind of change to the way we view her sacrifice, and also the sacrifice of our Lord. Hadn't she overruled both the Father and the Son before, in the second chapter of St. John's gospel? Could she not have again summoned this power, if it had been her desire?

This brings us to the heart of the matter. The greatest moment of pleasure, the greatest pleasure in history. The Theotokos, looking at her bloody and naked Son hanging on the cross, stretched and shredded (St. John 19:25). Before He was even born, she made the decision that would bring Him to that point. There was no joy in that moment, but there was pleasure. No joy, but unbounded love and peace. Salvation.

To be firmly planted in the will of God is the definition of the word "pleasure" for a Christian, and this is the test that links Christianity and pleasure. Indeed, the Theotokos knew this pleasure many, many times throughout her life. The crucifixion was the culmination of that journey.

*   *   *

O God let me stand behind her and look at her expression. She looks at her Son dying on the cross and she knows she has gained the desires of her heart. Let me learn from her face how pleasure cannot be captured in any moment, should not be, how that the moments of greatest pleasure are fleeting, how that often we even hope that they would pass quickly. Let me see how she has chosen this, and

He too. The will of God to suffer for the world. Let me, too, choose to define my joy according to the will of God for me and through me. Amen.

Fr. David R. Smith

Bibliography

1. **Bloom, Metropolitan Anthony.** *Courage to Pray.* New York: St. Vladimir's Seminary Press, 1997.

2. **Climacus, St. John.** *The Ladder of Divine Ascent.* Boston: Holy Transfiguration Monastery, 1979.

3. **Epicurus,** *Letter to Menoeceus.* Translated by Robert Drew Hicks. http://www.etext.library.adelaide.edu.au.

4. **Florensky, Pavel.** *Iconostasis.* Translated by Donald Sheehan and Olga Andrejev. New York: St. Vladimir's Seminary Press, 1996.

5. **Palmer, G.E.H., Philip Sherrard and Kallistos Ware, trans. and ed.** *The Philokalia: The Complete Text (Volume 2).* Compiled by St. Nicodemos of the Holy Mountain and St. Makarios of Corinth. London: Faber and Faber, Ltd, 1981

6. **Scupoli, Lorenzo.** *Unseen Warfare, Being the Spiritual Combat and Path to Paradise of Lorenzo Scupoli.* Edited by St. Nicodemus of the Holy Mounatin. Revised by Theophan the Recluse. Translated from Russian by E. Kadloubovsky and GEH Palmer. London: Faber and Faber, Ltd, 1952